*Public Sorrows and Private Pleasures*

*Studies in Phenomenology and*
*Existential Philosophy*

# WILLIAM EARLE

◇ ◇ ◇ ◇

# Public Sorrows
# and Private Pleasures

*Indiana University Press*

BLOOMINGTON AND LONDON

Chapter 1 was originally published in *The Monist*, vol. 56, no. 4 (Oct. 1972). Chapter 2 was originally published in *Ethics*, vol. 80, no. 4 (July 1970). Chapter 3 was originally published in *Conscientious Actions: The Revelation of the Pentagon Papers*, ed. Peter A. French (Cambridge, Mass.: Schenkman, 1973). Chapter 4 was originally published in *The Monist*, vol. 57, no. 4 (Oct. 1973). Chapter 5 was originally published in *Noonday, No. 1*, ed. Cecil Hemley (New York: Noonday Press, 1958). Chapter 6 was originally published in *Philosophy Forum*, vol. XI, ed. Ruben Gotesky (New York: Gordon and Breach, 1973). Chapters 7 and 10 were originally delivered for the Taft Lectureship, University of Cincinnati, 1971.

*For* JIM EARLE

# CONTENTS

# PREFACE

THE PUBLIC SORROWS discussed in the first part of this collection are recent and yet only repeat the movements of mind developed in Hegel's *Phenomenology of Mind.* They offer thereby contemporary illustration of the theses of that great book. But here my interest is not so much in any scholarly question as in tracing dramatically the fates of various gusts of passionate ideology that have swept the popular mind during the last decade and that are destined to sweep it forever. My method is dramatic or dialectical; that is to say, by provisionally adopting the spirit of some movement, I trace out the logical consequences so long as it remains faithful to itself. The sorrows result from the inherent shortcomings of the attitude adopted; they are one and all disastrous, not merely in thought but, more importantly, in life.

My chief effort is to disengage the *principle* of the attitude, that from which its many consequences flow, some of them comic, some pitiful, others deeply tragic. These consequences, documented daily by the newspapers, are in part determined by fashion, but more centrally by that inherent determining principle; the particular dress the ideological activity wears could be changed and already is changing. And yet those changes are themselves in their meaning strictly determined by the principle of the attitude, its essence. Substantial change would be only a change of principle.

The first essay looks at the radical; what on earth is behind the passion to "dismantle the establishment" in order to reconstruct a new one? What is the dramatic fate of any such desire? Why should anyone have ever supposed that formulas of *abstract* justice could in their immediate application be just? If the radical is seen as maddened by abstractions, the next essay looks at the sincere man of private conscience. He may be Thoreau or today's preacher or social scientist; what entitles such a man to overthrow tradition, law, or the public conscience? The Ellsberg case provides an illustration; it has of course been thrown out of the courts; but have the real issues been considered? Closely allied is the passion for pacifism: has this lovely ideology anything whatsoever in its favor beyond a somewhat sentimental desire to live the Kingdom of Heaven on earth?

If public life and thought have deteriorated under these insistences, their possible culture has also deteriorated under a technological passion to bring everything under a special rule or method. Do not all those activities of the spirit that have their only sense in a mutual *cooperation*, art, religion, and philosophy lose every vestige of their original meaning in professional separation? The death of culture is this spiritual disintegration into expertise.

Culture thus dies into civilization. There are reasons why no serious culture can endure; dialectically it *must* civilize itself, that is, reflect upon its own intents and pleasures. Civilization is here considered as a necessary moment in the life of the public mind, the inherent desire to blow up the whole of cultural seriousness into examination and amusement. But then the joke lasts too long, and what is the fate of civilization except a final, private recuperation of the spirit altogether beyond civilization?

That recuperation lies in the domain of private pleasures, the pleasures of the weary but transcendental mind. If these pleasures are to address themselves to the most serious interests of the spirit, I will call them "philosophical." But the name is not important. Art is an ultimate medium of what in another age might be called "philosophy." That the arts have this seriousness and can in effect *present* to the mind what philosophy has frequently taken to be a matter of argument is the burden of one essay; the arts can do all, and from one angle do it more perfectly for us than any philosophical argument that *separates* itself from aesthetic intuition. Surrealism certainly is the apocalypse of the philosophical imagination, and nothing could be more mistaken than to dismiss it as one more "aesthetic" movement of the twenties. It lives in that domain above the aesthetic and the philosophical, which could make both more serious and more available for our purposes the life of philosophical imagination at last!

Two final essays revert to *interiority* as the final destiny of each person. If the problems of the public have their public importance and if the public in the last analysis is no one, where is that one to whom it must all make a difference if it is to make any at all, and where indeed but in the final interiority of each? That subjectivity, considered *as it is for itself*, that is, in its interiority and singularity, must be the final origin and end of value if there is to be any. And yet, each person most usually is denounced as "merely" himself; the function of the last two essays is to remove the idea of "merely" and return not only the value but the philosophical sense of an otherwise unsurveyable domain of problems to where it should never have left: the transcendental and mystic life of the first-person singular.

*Public Sorrows and Private Pleasures*

# Part 1
## PUBLIC SORROWS:
## IDEOLOGY

# One

◇◇◇

# *The Radical Madness*

*For Eliseo Vivas*

TODAY, HAPPILY, we have much less confidence than a Montesquieu or a Hegel in depicting the "spirits" of nations, times, and generations. The more intelligible such depictions are and the more suitable for their role in world-historical drama, the less plausible they seem to those whose spirits they are supposed to be. For no matter how subtly drawn and with no matter how many reservations, they remain in the end *categories*. The application of categories to anything living itself generates a categorial malaise: the category is clear, but life, while it illustrates that category, also illustrates its opposite as well as an indefinite number of other categories not encompassed in either the one or the other.

If this error seems too obvious to mention, it is, I am convinced, the abstract statement of something whose resolute and systematic commission constitutes the spirit of the *radical*. In characterizing and criticizing such a spirit, this chapter might then seem to fall under its own condemnations; but it should be understood at the start that we shall be considering not persons, which would be indecent and personal, but persons *insofar as* they have chosen to radicalize themselves— or, put otherwise, only persons in their chosen roles, in the categories or personae they wish to illustrate. It will be therefore a categorial critique of categories, and not a categorial critique of persons. That ontological distinction preserves the dignity of the person while permitting a critique of his actions and aims. It is precisely the refusal to sustain such a distinction that constitutes the inherent confusion, distress, and ultimate futility of the radical position. This is said by way of preface and postface; in between I shall take a look at various facets of a contemporary moral distress called the "Movement" or the "Revolution," by analysis show it up as an absolute philosophical nullity and, when put into action, the father of atrocities.

To claim this distress as "contemporary" means here that it is remarkable in only a small section of our contemporaries, those who are either on campuses or who otherwise would be on them if they had not alienated themselves, a group so small they would properly go unnoticed if the newspapers did not from time to time announce yet another bombing by the Weathermen, or yet another atrocity committed under drugs, of which Manson and his "family" may stand for the *ne plus ultra*. The shocked public learns that what would otherwise be ascribed to madness instead offers an ideological explication and justification of itself: we are asked to look at a new "religion" or a new "politics," and even give Constitutional comfort to them. Are they not radical forms of Freedom? And who is there to speak a word against Freedom, unto the final freeing of oneself from the human condition altogether? In any event, we shall be looking at its "theory" or rather ideology if that term is taken as expressing a welter of slogans, sensibilities, associations, loves, and hatreds all rendered in a jargon that changes week by week. In passing, it might be noted that the ephemeral jargonization of speech follows a certain internal necessity of the Movement; no one can follow it without being in it, and to follow it is to follow nothing but the turbid movement itself; its jargon *says* nothing but does serve to distinguish the current members from the interested outsiders. And, of course, nothing is better designed to frustrate the "fascism of thought" than a radical confusion of language. The contemporary moral scene was not created by the youths who follow it but rather by their slightly senior intellectuals who hoped to find their audience in youth, and in

that were not disappointed. In this respect college students
have willingly played the role of Ion the Rhapsode to some
mad Homers. But let us begin our diagnosis.

## Some Phenomena

The radical, of course, is one who goes straight to the heart
or roots of everything and envisions some form of total
revolution. Now the revolution cannot be total unless what is
revolved turns upon one center; if the Establishment is to be
dismantled, it must be seen as a vast noxious outgrowth of a
single cause or, at least, a small number of manageable causes.
For if the whole of social life and its arrangements had no
single root, how could it be uprooted? If, in short, human life
were something which had an infinite number of roots in the
past, present, and presumptive future, if it were unsurveyable
in its sources and consequences, if men were not the puppets
of single passions, in a word, if concrete life were concrete life,
on what could the radical aim his guns? The reformer contents
himself with this or that change; the radical scorns the
reformer for trying to fight the hated Gorgon by cutting off
only a few heads; the radical goes straight to the heart of the
monster to kill it, which presupposes what is patently false,
that the historical social life of men is like Gorgon. The
fantastic notion that any existing society or even a single
person can be grasped altogether, in its "root," which can then
be extirpated or changed in essence, is the presupposition of
the radical's thought, his *proton pseudos*. And it is one form of
that logical error noted earlier, a form of the hubris of reason,
overconfident in its power of apprehension. It has some
particular forms I will now examine.

### THE MORALIZATION OF LIFE

Perhaps the initial and determining experience of the radical
is that society as a whole is immoral, immoral in its root. Or if
"immoral" is too redolent of a past age, "unjust," "intolerable," "repressive," or whatever term seems appropriate, but I
shall use "immoral." It is absolutely wrong and wrong in its

very roots; if the radical did not have some such consciousness of himself, the one who had unmasked a radical evil, how could he justify himself? Without his conviction, he would sink in his own eyes to what he is in the eyes of others, a common criminal. In a word, the radical is an implacable moralist, and his speech is that of denunciation. All of which is particularly astonishing considering the efforts of previous social science to de-moralize everything. The "historical sense," "cultural relativism," "ethnology," had all worked out, it thought, a benign pluralism which sympathetically entertained a variety of cultures, styles of life, values, and human destinies, which abstained from moral denunciations of human life, held the old missionaries in contempt, and hoped to promulgate a smiling and civilized interest in everything. Nothing could be more abhorrent to its heart than Jeremiah denouncing the people for wickedness and calling for a radical change of heart. No sooner said and done, than all undone in the moralism of the fifties and sixties, when Jeremiah shouts again. Savanarola burnt wicked books and the frivolities of personal adornment; following the same necessities, the radicals too shun personal adornment and, as for books, when they are not burned they are simply not read. If before, the deluded prophets spoke in the name of God, their successors, equally confident of their insight, speak from the chair of social justice and freedom.

One mark of the most primitive thought is its penchant for tracing the most diverse phenomena back to a single cause or spirit; but there is no need of anthropology for our best examples. The contemporary radicals serve far better: from the most trivial to the most terrifying "evils," they are one and all traced back to that root which they wish to extirpate. What is its name? No one knows, or rather its names are legion: imperialism, racism, private property, exploitation, repression, technology, a bad relation to "Nature," and so on, ending finally with "it all. . . ." And the phenomena of immorality or injustice? From smoking cigarettes, driving an automobile, eating fruit sprayed with detergent or grapes gathered by nonunion workers, through either traveling or not traveling to North Vietnam, China, or the Soviet Union, paying the income tax, failing to stir up students on these questions or teaching at all at a university, to the horrors of patriotism, respect for policemen, the flag, until we reach the ultimate symptom of all moral rot, our efforts in Indochina.

Now my present point is not to discuss any of these particular issues, but to note the aegis under which the new radical discusses them: they are all moral symptoms of a deeper moral flaw, which itself must be rooted out lock, stock, and barrel. It is not enough to address oneself to anything specific; that would be superficial. It is that potent but unnameable spirit behind all of this which is the Enemy. The Enemy, as in the most primitive thought, lives in some vague exteriority; it is rarely in oneself, although outsiders hear reports of sessions where radicals rap and examine their own hearts; with the pitiful sincerity of children, they ask themselves how they may have unwittingly sinned that week, maybe even shaken hands with the Enemy!

The immediate consequence of the moralization of every problem, and the accompanying devil theory of human life is the abrupt and irremediable termination of the political process. To make a pact with the devil is itself devilish, and since the political process is essentially devoted to discussion, compromise, and mutual adjustments of claims and convictions, the political process itself must disappear into revolution. Politics is effective only when the parties to the process respect one another, regard the other not as immoral but as differently moral and have sufficient faith in the society as a whole to give up something personal for its success. But if society as a whole is the Enemy, and if opponents are unjust, repressive, fascists, in a word, immoral, what basis is there for discussion or agreement?

It is hardly surprising, then, that even the feeblest of radical devices far short of assassination and bombing are all deteriorations of any genuine political process. Since the radical is not likely to be effective with legitimate representatives of the citizens, he will favor the "people," which means citizens are unrepresented, that is, the mob. Up goes a new slogan, "power to the people," a singularly hypocritical one to be immediately withdrawn if the "people" form themselves into a lynching bee or even a crowd of angry hard-hats. And then there is the device of civil disobedience, thought to be ennobled by the examples of Thoreau and Gandhi, in which disobedience is taken to be obedience to a higher moral law, conscience, or conscience speaking the judgments of the radical press; it is not long before some expect to be rewarded for their disobedience to the laws by the laws themselves. That civil disobedience is simply a refusal to comply with those laws and hence *must* be punished by the laws is forgotten, particularly when society out of weariness or indifference in turn looks upon the disobedient as pranksters or misguided hotheads. And some have carried their ideas to the point where they are willing to dissolve the historical units of society, dreaming of separate political states for themselves, usually California, which would issue visas, admit some and refuse admission to others, maybe a black state or a pot state, and of course, in its new sovereignty, endowed with the power to make war. Or maybe a city community within a city, with its own laws, police force, and mayor. The radical radicals perceive the folly of all this; they have world and even metaphysical ambitions analogous to the god Shiva, who created and destroyed worlds at will: no *small* communities for them.

With the radical moralization of life comes the concomitant modification of human discourse. We have already noticed the preference for a slang that changes so fast no outsider can keep up; nor any insider either, since it is deliberately designed to *say* nothing but only to stir sympathies and antipathies, in effect to create a subconscious emotional group. But moralists of whatever stamp rarely have anything to *say* anyway; their speech is denunciation and persuasion, and all under a rock-solid conviction of being right. Among moralists then there can be no discussion, only rant; neither side has or can have anything to learn from the other, since learning is not exactly the forte of those who have achieved absolute insight. Naturally, nothing could be more common then than the wail that the older generation does not "listen" to them. "Listen," like so many radical terms, has taken on its opposite sense, namely, "agree with." But if "agreement" is now the precondition of discussion, it is hard to know what discussion genuinely discusses. Herbert Marcuse won't even permit much of that in his new state, where what had always been called "intolerance" is now gleefully redubbed "repressive tolerance," the emphasis as always falling upon "repressive."

Or, lacking the capacity for discussion, the radicals are willing from time to time to *rap* or *dialogue*. This at first sight looks admirable; it even suggests genuine discussion, until disillusion sets in. The moralist and radical really have nothing to discuss, and the dialoguing will show it. First of all, everyone of no matter what age must sit on the floor, so that no one is "higher" than anyone else. Have we not seen pictures of aged college presidents sitting on the floor or wishing to be beneath the rug in order to show to all their common spirit? But not merely must everyone be on the floor, all minds and ideas also must sit there. Again we are the spectators of the Grand Simplification, an equalization in which the experienced and the young, the informed and uninformed, the young and the old, the loud and the quiet, all must be equalized; or not exactly; those tainted with the bad vibes of experience must be equalized *out*. The genuinely dialoguing group will not dig them; and if they try to reason, to consider alternatives, realities, they are definitely not with it. Gut-feeling is the word, yet who can *feel* thought, experience, and reason? Do they not even give rise to the suspicion that one is being exploited by the "fascism of the mind"? "Thinking" is indeed suspect in dialoguing; its worst sin perhaps is introducing a pause between certain conviction and action. Even Herbert Marcuse's books are no longer read; they do not "propel the reader into the streets" but waste his time thinking. None of this would have surprised Hegel, of course, who knew and perfectly analyzed these frenzied phenomena of "conscience" and the "heart" as final arbiters of action.

And so: all of life falls under an abstract moral judgment, and the moral glow that judges is that which finds all of it, subsumed under the idea of the Establishment, wicked. The organ that accomplishes this monstrous judgment is called the "heart" or "conscience." Political process and discussion are replaced by no process at all but the immediacy of bombings, civil disobedience, assassinations, shoutings at street rallies; discussion, with its own sense of both relevance and irrelevance, is replaced by dialoguing, where digging, feelings, vibes among the sympathetic hold sway. After all, the moral is always the conclusive if not convulsive; he who loves conclusions would only waste his time with considerations, whose only effect, as he experiences them, is to cool moral passion. But a cool moral passion is none at all; it even begins to look like the proper basis of intelligence, civilization and accommodation.

### THE CATEGORICAL ELIMINATION OF EXPERIENCE: THE METHOD OF YOUTH

The radical moralist necessarily *judges;* he is the judge *par excellence.* What indeed would be the point of moralizing if one could not judge with a resounding "guilty!"? Judgment is an essential function of the human spirit, of course; but for our present purpose we can note two very different forms: the unconditional and the conditional. The unconditional judgment immediately subsumes the act or institution under an ideal abstraction of justice, equality, or whatever; no wonder that this form of judgment is usually condemnatory, uncompromising, and pitiless. It is the form of judgment beloved of the radical spirit to which anything else looks wishy-washy and sold-out. It obviously requires nothing by way of experience; the abstract ideal is lodged a priori within the abstract conscience and is unquestionable; the act or institution judged demands only a minimum of acquaintance to exhibit its distance from the ideal; nothing is simpler than unconditional condemnation. And it is obvious at a glance why such judgments can easily proliferate throughout the world; the Establishment, the Power Structures all fall instantly under its condemnation with a persuasiveness that captivates all who have little experience of life.

The conditional judgment also decides, but it has another domain within which it is deciding, namely, an ambiguous world. Now, to know that the world is ambiguous requires experience, and not the experience of the cynics but that of responsible men, with memory to recall how often they have been wrong themselves before their own judgment, and how often things and persons have turned different faces to them in time. Nothing could be more repulsive to such a spirit than the unconditional judgment, the immediacy with which a simple radical spirit holds each thing in isolation, or all of them together, up to an abstract ideal. Experience is the very medium of the conditional judgment, and since it is what youth does not have, youth is given to the radical and unconditional. And so with the "intellectuals," who are not intellectual *by virtue* of their experience in life but by virtue of intellectual powers independent of it, powers of abstraction, analysis, dialectic, argumentation. Now these virtues are indeed virtues, but not exactly those required for conditional, practical moral judgment.

The unconditional judgment with its categorical elimination of experience dictates a certain *way* of pronouncing judgment. Classical literature abounds in examples of judges, even God Himself, who, while they must pronounce judgment, do so with a tear in their eye. The ultimate origin of that tear would carry us far beyond the scope of these remarks, and yet it could hardly be in that radical and unconditional spirit which, confident in its apprehension of absolute good and evil, is pitiless in its condemnation of the world. And if some freshly experienced pitilessness appears to radicals as a new and rigorous hardness, to others it looks like hatred masking as moralism, and I shall have to be forgiven if I no longer know which is the origin of which. But all of this, deeply explored in the *Bhagavad Gita*, the Old and New testaments, and virtually every place where men who knew something of life reflected upon themselves, no doubt equally appears as a digression into conventional sentimentalism to the radical spirit. Precisely why, that spirit asks, should one shed a tear for "those who cause" war, inequality, slavery, exploitation, oppression, and the rest? Is that tear not a sign of personal weakness, perhaps a first trace of the softening of the radical will? In any case, it is usually called "humanity," and most assuredly it is that humanity which is the final enemy of the new radical tyrants, moralists devoid of experience. The unconditional judgment abstracts a man, his acts, or a society and its institutions from concrete conditions, and holds it up before the abstract moral category; the "conditions," however, happen to be *essential* to the truth of any judgment about existence, existence itself being the domain of conditions which are unsurveyable. No wonder the essential error built into the radical spirit. Its essential mercilessness follows necessarily.

The radical, youthful moralist following his own lights proceeds to make himself a tyrant. Tyrants notoriously have always had to "make themselves *hard,*" that is, by a secret inner act turn themselves into unpersons. The shedding of humanity, first inwardly and then shamelessly before the world, is the very essence of the despot. Popular history records mostly the shocking and the unprecedented; but who enacts such unheard-of deeds but unprecedented men? And who are they but those who are the most radical, that is, those who have freed themselves of what had been regarded as the "human" until themselves? It is certainly not an accident that those who choose to turn themselves into something unprecedented exercise their first radical critique upon precedents, either with only an inkling of what tradition is or in an abysmal ignorance of it, or through a pathological withdrawal of respect for what had until themselves passed as the human. A *new age* will begin with themselves, and with that their historical place is guaranteed, at least in the popular histories of monsters.

The new age indeed looks new for a moment, the moment it originates. There must at the beginning be a new simplification. Human beings are now radically reclassified: people are divided with ease into sheep and goats; they are either with us or else they are "hyenas," "pigs," or excrement. It is now for the first time relatively easy to decide who are *worthy* of life. For those who survive the first test, actions are easy to command or proscribe categorically, always on the most formal grounds. Their arts, religions, and philosophies are quickly subsumed under immediate judgments. They are "degenerate," "socially dangerous," or "useless," "bourgeois," "parasitic," and so on, all seen through those steely eyes that never betrayed the least glint of recognition of what humans, their acts, and their final ambiguous tragedies and loves ever were. Nor was any such thing ever necessary; after all, was this

not to be a *new* age, a wiping of the slate clean, somethin
unprecedented? The "slate" that is being wiped clean, ·the
human spirit and its historical social life, is being wiped clean
of precisely that traditional singular experience that is not the
possession of "anyone," but that into which we slowly find our
places, which is what we are and have lived, and is the very
medium of any significantly human life, as well as any
significant judgment of it; it is precisely that which the radical
spirit has chosen to detest. The resulting tabula rasa, for
whatever philosophical curiosity it has elicited in epistemologi-
cal questions as a spiritual prime matter, is certainly denuded
of every capacity for either understanding or recreating
anything recognizably human. It would, if possible, be indeed
unprecedented.

The radical spirit, denuded of that tradition and experience
which could only erode its radicality, can, of course, only
exercise the unconditional and abstract judgment: right or
wrong, good or bad, yes or no, for us or against us, preserve or
eliminate; in a word, like a fish in water, it lives in the medium
of the unconditional moral judgment. It breathes only in those
judgments which other men who do not wish to make
themselves unprecedented in the continuous history of humanity shun at all costs from making, and to whose necessity they
succumb only at the *extremity*, when they must. Hence it is
not surprising that for the radical moralist, *everything is a
crisis*, or can gleefully be made into one. Where before, there
were requests, now there are nonnegotiable demands. Meetings become confrontations full of sass, impudence, and
effrontery. Courtesy vanishes into incivility. Every trace of the
*ancien régime* must be obliterated categorically, and, since the
*ancien régime* was indeed a whole society and form of life,
there can never be an occasion when hostility is not appropriate. The ensuing bewilderment and counter-hostility among
those still living in the previous age is of course only a new
source of glee to the new men. New words must be substituted
for old, new values, new behavior, new clothes, and new faces,
eyes now inscrutable behind black glasses. The new man
wishes to become unrecognizable; his virtues will seem like
vices to former men, his language incoherent to them, his

behavior mad or childish, in a word, an effort to abruptly create a new world out of nothing. At first, it simply looks like the emergence of the dregs of the former world; but the new man intends to reverse such judgments by dominance; they are not dregs but prophets.

It hardly takes much perspicacity to perceive that *no such unconditional counter-world is possible.* What *is* possible is a change of personnel and a temporary confusion, a deterioration of custom, precedent, expectation, a redistribution of wealth, honors, and power all in this world. But the new age when installed proceeds to reinstitute all those a priori structures and hierarchies it thought it was destroying, and who is surprised when those new, unprecedented, and faceless men gradually become old, begin to cherish their personal faces and uniforms, plaster them on billboards everywhere, prefer their old revolutionary friends or execute them, establish new precedents and rules suspiciously like the old? The revolutionary work has produced nothing but a vast and temporary dust-storm of confusion. A small change here or there, most usually one that was already afoot during the previous age.

Survivors into the new age might even welcome the restoration of social order, precedent, and tradition if they could ever quite forget the blood shed to give the wheel another delusive turn. It may be questioned whether it is in the least possible for history to move "forward"; but is there any question at all whether it should move forward at this cost? In any event, if the "progress" of history must be at the expense of "cracked heads," must we not always ask on *what scale* the "progress" is being measured? It might be theoretically possible to "progress" clear outside the human precedent itself by relentlessly pursuing something that appears to its devotees as "unconditionally moral."

The dialectic of the radical spirit I have been trying to trace has its own phenomenological logic. It is by no means a casual, empirical summary of current fads and fantasies, which have been sufficiently documented by others. The radical spirit, even when it thinks itself most free, is in effect, *when consistent*, the servant of an idea. It is that idea whose puppet he is that directs the radical's attitudes; his only freedom, as a human being, is whether and how to follow it. If we can grasp, then, the determining idea of the radical spirit, we shall have grasped that essence from which the sequence of the radicals' passions and actions follow, when their meaning is understood. And the truth of that analysis would, of course, be quite independent of what the radical thinks he is doing, but would enable us to understand even the peculiarities of that thought, though not in its own terms.

The radical spirit has fallen in love with an abstraction, the abstract moral idea; since the moral idea is moral, it of itself commands its immediate realization in history. And so the radical spirit must necessarily attempt to introduce into history and life a perfect abstraction. If it merely contemplated its abstraction, it would be morally remiss in its devotions, and contemptible in its own eyes. Any abstract ideal whatsoever can enter history only by way of a revolution in that history; and, if the abstract ideal preserves its abstract purity, the revolution it generates must be *perpetual*. That pure or abstract ideals must necessarily generate a perpetual revolution within history is a consequence of the ontological difference between existence and ideal abstraction. They are two ontological domains with radically different properties; their immediate fusion is catastrophe or revolution, a writhing of existence when it is touched even for a moment by the abstract or ideal. History, of course, has its *own* practical ideals, which are *never* abstract; it moves accordingly in its own concrete way, adjusting itself to its own changes. But such movement is never revolutionary, never directed by abstractions, and it always manages to preserve some continuity of social and personal substance. It would therefore be a monstrous mistake to suppose that individuals and societies not maddened by abstractions must sink into apathy, have no moral life at all, and finally die; *that* is an illusion cultivated by the radical, and it expresses no reality except the profound blindness of the radical spirit.

A glance at the fundamental ontological difference between abstract ideal and historical existence is sufficient to see the essence of what is characteristic of the radical spirit and its favorite activities. Abstract ideals, liberty, equality, fraternity, rights, happiness, justice—the list is endless—all have the common property of being *ideas*. They are ideas of the Good, what reason itself can perceive of the Good. As the abstractive work of reason, they must bear all the signs of that work; after all, not everything that passes through the mind is an *idea*. Experiences, passions, memories, none of these can be called "ideas" in our present sense. The marks of an idea are simplicity, clarity, distinctness. "Equality" possesses an almost mathematical clarity; "Freedom" is particularly clear since it is nothing but the negative idea of being independent of everything else. "Justice" at first glance seems equally simple and clear, perceptible to the untutored reason in every man. And "Happiness" looks like the very obvious sense of life; is there anyone who would defend "unhappiness"? Each, inspected by reason or "conscience," is in itself clear, and distinct from its opposites, which are all various forms of Evil. The satisfactions possible to an idealism of this stamp are endless and quite understandable. In the first place, ideas do not demand experience for their comprehension since they have been abstracted from that problematic and questionable domain. They are in their rational simplicity equally available to all. The simplest and most naive heart can pretend to love them. They are democratic *par excellence*. From which we deduce their popularity with the young. All of them, in their capacity of being "moral," command at first glance *immediate realization;* they are so many trumpet calls for action. Again, their appeal to the active young is obvious. An idea, as such, stands alone; it is distinct from its opposite; it has no history, no precedents, no context except logical or dialectical; it neither knows nor can know anything of precisely that domain of historical existence where it wishes to intrude. When it does so intrude, it is hardly surprising that it can do so only by perpetually turning that existence upside down, by the perpetual revolution. For no sooner is a new historical formation created, than it too falls under radical criticism. It too is but another historical, existential formation, necessarily sharing all the faults of existence as such when held up against the purely abstract. Hence the true radical revolutionary is, unknown to himself, fighting against ontological necessities and must necessarily fail.

It is hardly a controversial philosophical thesis that the very essence of what we call existence is to be infinitely various, infinitely ambiguous, and infinitely incapable of being thoroughly grasped. It is apprehended through finite points of view, perspectives, glimpses, opinions, all of which declare their incompleteness of themselves. Now, how indeed can any such thing as existence, whether it is that of one man or of a society, let alone the history of men, offer itself up to any such thing as the abstract ideal, instantly graspable by anyone in its own unique clarity, simplicity, and distinctness? *Of course* our lives, their precedents, and their destinies are over our heads; the refusal to live in such a domain by submitting it all to the pseudo-clarity of the idea is precisely the choice of the ideological radical. As G. K. Chesterton remarked, the madman is not he who has lost his reason, but he who has lost everything but his reason.

The Good itself, which secretly animates the whole process giving its own majesty and ultimacy to each of its infinite forms—justice, equality, fraternity, freedom—the Good itself appears somewhat remote, in the same position as God the Father, too awful to approach except in more human forms, which adapt themselves to the circumstances of their devotees. And to any dialectician worth his salt, nothing could be clearer than the proposition that from the Good itself *nothing whatsoever in particular* can possibly follow. It cannot direct conduct, it is the goal of no action, and it can neither criticize nor justify anything whatsoever. Which is not to deny its meaning, but to locate that meaning elsewhere, out of the field of political or personal decision. It must remain behind and out of sight for the political and moral practices of men. Appeals to it can only wreak havoc with decision and the political process, when men are most clearheaded and responsible about their direct concerns.

The various epiphanies of the Good are not much better. Each *specifies* the Good: equality is not the same as fraternity, nor either the same as freedom, nor any the same as justice,

nor any of these the same as excellence. Even in their relative
abstractness they are all *specifications* of that highest principle, the Good. As specifications, each delimits itself from the
others; what one all by itself demands is refused by another.
To refer or allude to them for ultimate justification then is not
to solve a problem but to create one. Or rather to reflect, now
in the ideal domain, precisely that ambiguity and pluralism of
meanings and values which essentially define the domain of
life. It is apparent, therefore, that there can never be any
situation at all in existence that is undiscussable, nonnegotiable, and unable to withstand the political process, instead to be
solved by "dismantling the Establishment," "cracking heads"
as though they were eggs for an omelette, closing down the
governmental institutions made to assist the political process,
exploding bombs, or joyfully committing acts of treason. The
ironic horror of these dialectical errors is that the Good itself
or any of its abstract specifications can enter history immediately only through conspicuous evil. Nor could there be any
justification whatsoever for those forms of negotiation in which
the parties to the negotiation are committed to contempt for
one another. If the immediate introduction of the abstract
ideal into history is a form of contempt for living history itself,
its agent, the radical spirit, also imagines a certain ideal aura
about his head, the aura of contempt for existing life. He loves
the "charismatic," is prepared for or even desires martyrdom;
he has an unprecedented life, something more than human, or,
in other eyes, less. Inflamed by the abstract, he pays the price
by sacrificing that life to the abstract, accomplishing whatever
of value he might accomplish only at random, by accident, and
as a by-product of his ultimately metaphysical revolt. It would
not be difficult to make comparisons with artistic "geniuses" of
the Wagnerian stamp, possessed by their Muse, and therewith
authorized to do as· they wished; but where this may be
"interesting" in the arts, it is little short of a horror in political
existence. The confusion of aesthetic with moral categories
that Kierkegaard exposed in its absolute depth continues to
generate new tragedies, in which the radical spirit lives not so
much in the presence of God as in that of news media and
dreams of his own role in posthumous histories; what he has

forgotten and where he misfires is precisely that domain, human existence, where his true function should have been envisaged in the first place.

The alternative to all this has already been adumbrated. It will look "immoral" to the radical fanatic, but not especially noteworthy to men of some practical experience and responsibility in life, since it is what they do anyway and by sound instinct. The alternative to the theoretical life of the radical is not, needless to say, yet another theory or ideology, which would be no alternative at all. But the alternative begins with the realization that *no* sensible or wise decisions can proceed out of theory or of reasons that can be adequately stated. Reason, so understood, has always been the hallmark of the "theoretical man," and at the same time the source of his manic irrelevance to practical decision. Ideology may be appealing to the young and the intelligentsia, who rarely proceed from talk to practical decision, or, if they do, can only act violently. But it looks either foolish or insane to those who must both act and hold themselves responsible for the consequences. The truth is that the man quick with reasons is used only by practical men on public occasions to give easy rhetorical formulations for decisions made strictly on other grounds, grounds *always* too complex to state. The "intellectual" then "names" a decision already made or "argues" for it by subsuming it under some more or less popular moral category, whether "just" or "unjust." None of this, of course, has anything whatsoever to do with the pertinent thinking behind the decision. That thinking, if it has any seriousness at all, involves matters far too complex, far too embedded in experience, risk, and hope to ever be formulable. Political thinking when responsible is always within a schema of the whole, not so rigid as to be insensitive to its own limits, yet not so loose as to offer no direction. It must envisage schematically the whole of political life since political society is not an agglomeration of separable persons, classes, acts, or moments, but aims at least at a *whole society in movement*. Political decision then must not merely look at the simple question of "spending more for health," but also know that spending more for health is spending less for defense, welfare, education, and the rest. Analogously, a physician would be incompetent if he treated one organ at the expense of the others, eventually the organism. Nor is an organism a summation or agglomeration of organs, but a single living creature with a mind and purposes in life, a past and a presumptive future. The ideological doctor could only be a quack; reducing all illnesses to disorders of the spine, heart, diet, or elimination, he looks simpleminded. Taking over the whole patient and reforming his life radically, he is nothing but a tyrant of another, seeking to unmake the past, reconceive the present, and compose for his patient a life according to a scenario envisaged by himself. But physicians since Aesclepius have known perfectly well that their arts only assist the natural life of the body to maintain itself; it is not to generate monstrosities by favoring one organ, nor is it to produce a wholly new life by a magical art. If true physicians then humbly cooperate with a natural life already afoot, how could true political thinkers do otherwise in a domain even more complex and even less amenable to theory?

And so true political decision is circumspect; it involves that knowledge of the feasible which only experience can suggest, a sense of the time required, of what good may be lost with every new one chosen, a sense of alternatives, limitations, possibilities, a sense of continuity since it is only within continuous experience that experience itself can count for anything. All of this amounts to a patience which knows that not every evil in life is remediable by political action, and yet some are. Good political sense, the only one that can be effective, could be given an indefinite number of formulations; what those formulations aim at is indeed a sense and not an idea, and a sense is embodied only in a man of a given stamp. His "sense" is not in the least a dialectical expertise but something born of both experience and its experiential critique, involving abilities and experiences neither transferable nor teachable nor even comprehensible by that abstract reason which all possess as their birthright. To the radical spirit, obviously, these are the most questionable abilities of all; born out of historical life and pertinent only to it, they must be vulnerable to any abstract critique descending from the a priori; political wisdom as such seems forever compromised to that radical and abstract revolution against historical political life itself. Little wonder that political ability has little charm for the young and for those maddened by abstractions; it is beyond their reach, whereas abstract justice, equality, fraternity can be grasped in a flash by anyone, experienced or not, and with that flash the radical achieves the conclusion to all possible discussions.

In effect, then, the second phenomenon in the present moral distress is the frighteningly abstract character of the gods who have maddened the radical. Being abstract, they have no history, and they can enter history only through violence, and, being abstractly rational, they can have no truck with that slow, ambiguous, tentative yet stubborn *sense* of human affairs that defines political wisdom.

### HOW TO BECOME ALIENATED

There are friends, enemies, acquaintances, the indifferent, and then something else: the "alien." Has one ever heard so much talk before about "alienation"? With Hegel, as everyone who has read him knows, alienation as well as reconciliation take on their full metaphysical depth; but then the contemporary "alienated" cannot read Hegel. Their alienation would then appear as nothing more than a deplorable prolongation of an adolescent disease, except now it wishes to justify itself. Not merely are they alienated in some sense in which they ought to get over it, but they *ought* to be alienated, *everyone* ought to be alienated, and those who are not absolutely alienated are hypocrites. Society and everyone in it ought to be "restructured" so that the presently alienated would find themselves home at last.

The immodesty of the attitude needs no comment, but then modesty is only appropriate within a society recognized as a source of values within which one takes one's place and from which one draws a significant portion of the values of one's life and to which therefore loyalty and piety are appropriate. But no, all that belongs to the unreconstructed consciousness. Today is the day for a "rational critique of society." From what *standpoint* such a critique is to be operated is most obscure indeed, although for any ordinary mind it should be the first order of the day. What could be more obvious than that there *cannot be* any "rational critique" of society? Which is not to say that there can be no critique at all of it, but that that critique cannot proceed out of reason or anything remotely like it. Reason could conceivably only operate within society, clearing up this or that, finding more appropriate ways of doing things, extending the coherence of laws, eliminating patent injustices, and so forth; but for *reason* to wish to dismantle this society or create a new one is for it seriously to mistake its rightful powers, blinding itself in hubris to both its origins and its proper scope. What reason can do, clearly, is *to see*, to infer, to examine and illuminate. What it *cannot* do is to create anything, decide or choose anything. Even the choice to reason at all is itself not a choice by reason. And it follows that while reason certainly can find this incoherent with that, it cannot itself choose either coherence or incoherence. It is therefore in no authentic position to reconstruct anything whatsoever. It can do its best to *light up* choices but that is all; and there is a further serious question whether even this is not in principle too much for anything called reason. The previous section developed this theme. In any event, and for whatever it is worth, men have only very rarely chosen to live solely by the light of reason, have only very rarely chosen to rationalize their society, preferring always a more incoherent, flexible confusion of things to that tidy coherence which is all that is available to even the most subtle and comprehensive reason. Has not every rationalized society appeared before and afterward as nothing but a concealed tyranny? During its rise it lives on hope; when that hope begins to be fulfilled, the first cracks in the rational world appear.

Back to the alienated ones, for a moment conspicuous in urban centers throughout the world, wearing their new uniform of artificial rags, hair tangled in Gordian knots, faces sullen and morose, social gestures full of the uncertainty whether even to shake hands with the Enemy or not, perceiving hypocrisy everywhere, and confirming their aliena-tion by stealing rather than working, lying in order to play the Establishment's game, and living for as long as possible off the effluvia of affluence. Their favorite music is too loud to be listened to, a form of aural assault whose purpose is the obliteration of anything but the consciousness of itself. It is of course a sublime protest, but against what? And for what? But the latter question hardly bothers the alienated ones: "first the revolution, then we shall decide what we shall do. . . ." Against what? A certain embarrassment flushes the face when one hears the list of horrors against which the revolution revolts: a consumer society, television, Madison Avenue, alcohol, regular hours, marriage, wearing clothing at all, a conventional smile, private property, differentiations between male and female, teacher and student, young and old, rich and poor, white and black, or, in fact, the category of differentiation in any manifestation. Here the flower children of a few years back enacted in advance what the activists only vaguely dream about. All is One, the flower children saw, garlanding the police with wild posies. At least the flower children were not alienated, so long as they could float away into Lotus Land; it was waking up that did it. But the activists manage to maintain their alienation by a certain mental process I shall examine below. Not that there have not always been and always will be more than enough objects from which they may feel alienated. Still, perhaps all those objects have a single meaning: *authority!* It can be perceived everywhere: the obstinate authority of the past, and particularly the present, where authority can actually be seen and felt in the form of the police, professors, males, whites, the civilized, the President, parents, and so on virtually *ad infinitum.* Higher and Lower can be seen everywhere; is it not detestable, particularly to the Lower, and must therefore the revolution not be total and permanent? So it seems to the *Lumpenintelligenzen* who, although they call upon Nietzsche in their ignorance, fail to perceive that it was the *failure* of the Will to Power, the failure of discrimination, by which Nietzsche characterized the modern age of nihilism and vacuity. But such matters can hardly touch those who do not dig either reading or thought. But the paradise dreamed of by the alienated can hardly even be called "childish"; the blessed happiness of children, as we recollect it, was possible only under the protective wings of

the parents, and known to be so by every child worthy of the
name. No matter: the hubris of egalitarian Reason knows no
bounds, and who is to say whether even the most fundamental
conditions of humane existence could not be swept away,
leaving its scourges with what would be an unprecedented
desert. But of course even a minimal sense of existence is not
the strong point of the revolutionary moralists. The millennia
of human existence have exhibited in an infinite variety of
forms always the old basic conditions of hierarchy, authority,
and differentiations of role, taste, and style. Yet who is to say
that we cannot abolish authority forever? And lurking around
among the many hidden premises of that view is the most
dangerous one of all: if it *can* be done, it *should* be done, or at
least tried. The total lack of any existential anchoring in this
mad dream or rational critique need hardly be emphasized;
but perhaps what does deserve attention is the inevitable
paradox, known well to Hegel, that unanchored reason is in
fact not unanchored at all: it is simply blind to its own anchor,
which now in unexamined shape proceeds to exert its own
particular will. In the present case, alienated from society and
refusing to be the illuminating organ for society, the active
force of reason well hidden from reason itself turns out to be
nothing but a rather miserable form of *egotism*. It will speak
the language of reason, justice, democracy, and the Future;
but the organ speaking is the individual ego, which would
never have surprised Nietzsche. Where indeed is the hypocrisy?

Why then the alienation from society? Simply because
society is *there*, already alive and going; but where do *I* fit in?
It has to be sure, a place for me but the *I* may have a *higher*
one in the new society of which I can envisage nothing except
that in it *I* will be more loved, respected, and honored than
now. And, raving on, should there not be a *special* punishment
devised for the present happy few, some special humiliations
devised for the exploiters, expropriators, imperialists, racists,
those hated Authorities, who are the "cancer of history"?

The rage against Authority can like all spiritual phenomena
be understood in a multiplicity of ways both accidental and
essential. Here we shall content ourselves with a phenomeno-

logical understanding, that is, with an effort to articulate what that rage rages against as seen in reflection and not by itself, since rage never reflects and therefore has only a naive understanding of itself. In a word, we shall try to understand it better than it does itself, and not through any help from psychoanalysis or any genetic interpretation, which could never get at the *essence* of the lived phenomenon. How can the very *sense* of spiritual phenomena be disclosed by tracing any phenomena back to infantile manifestations, manifestations of what but the very phenomenon that seeks clarification? And so, for whatever value it might have, I do not perceive any great clarification of the rage against Authority to be found in prior rages against Father; if it is the same, where is the clarification; and if it is different, how does it help to clarify anything? Why indeed should anyone rage against Papa? And if one does, then what does that *mean?* We must return to the essence of the act itself.

To rage against Authority, first of all, is not a fatality but rather a *choice*. No one is *obliged* to do so either by way of early experience, genes, sex, minority in age, citizenship, or any *situation* whatsoever; nor is there any a priori obligation to do so that derives from the Good or any defensible moral principle whatsoever. The principle it most usually invokes is Freedom; but if the freedom in question is a freedom from authority, it is synonymous with anarchy, and anarchy as a guiding principle is on any level of being—from the atom on up through a thing, plant, animal, human being to a society—synonymous with the death of that unit. Since any entity is obviously a unity of parts, for each part to dissociate itself from the unity is for the unity to dissolve; but the dissolution can never stop if it proceeds ahead *on principle:* the so-called "part" is itself a unity of its own parts, each of which, claiming independence and freedom, now runs free, and itself becomes subject to the same ontological decomposition. If the process is arrested at any particular stage, the ordering and dominating principle that stops the disintegrating process is vulnerable to the charge from its parts that it is "authoritarian"; by what "right" indeed does it arrogate to itself the power to arrest universal disintegration?

If the rights of anarchy are preposterous, metaphysically understood, they are terrifying socially enacted. To refuse accreditation to social authority by the cultivation of alienation, under the madcap of freedom and equality, is of course to remove oneself either legally or inwardly from the fundamental basis of citizenship. I, as an individual, obviously am not free from the legal authority of those above me; nor am I "equal" to them in their office. To become alienated from Authority and from its consequent principle of hierarchy may sound exhilarating to the alienated ones, each of whom now feels himself superior to what is rejected; but the superiority is the superiority of the empty over the full, the indeterminate over the determinate, the possible over the actual. And now if the profoundly alienated, having experienced their elation, would begin to fill their void: create, for example, out of their own private and untutored imaginations something called a society, moreover a society with its own traditions, rules, and expectations, and then a new language, new and unheard-of thoughts, or a vast and unsurveyable past of the arts, sciences, and social custom, in short, if they would complete their work, they might have the chilling experience of the vapidity of their project as well as the insufficiency of their means. To command others to divest themselves of authority, hierarchy, direction, control, as well as the civilization possible only under such circumstances, ranges from the criminal to the childishly foolish. Acceptance of authority and hierarchy, both political and cultural, is of course the beginning both of wisdom and of any informed freedom that could be useful to either the individual or his society.

### ON MAKING ONESELF MISERABLE

We now have before our eyes three phenomena, or rather three faces of a single phenomenon: a group of intellectual contemporaries who have chosen to turn themselves into moralists of society; who have chosen to think with the least appropriate tools for even such unsmiling tasks as moral judgment, abstractions of conscience rather than concrete sense, experience, and piety; and who finally, or perhaps at the very start, have adopted the attitude of alienation as the only one morally justified. A mad circle indeed and open to anyone who wishes to adopt it. Happily there are other honorable ways to live.

But to return to our theme, if the present radical generation finds itself morally distressed, it has *made* itself so, and this observer would like to add "too bad." There are and always will be concrete effective things to do either to maintain or to improve society, but the hysterically alienated moralist is not exactly in a position to do them. What is more pitiful than the tear-stained faces of young demonstrators when, a week or so after the demonstration, everything has remained the same? And what more depressing than the opposite reaction to these exercises in futility, the radical become cynical? If you can't beat them, join them; and the "them" he joins not by accident turn out to be the least responsible members of society, those "self-seekers" the radical used to see everywhere, where they were and where they were not.

There remains the question of phenomenological motive: why does consciousness choose something like the attitude sketched? To ask *it* is useless: it will only repeat the selected list of real or imagined ills, whose evil "justifies" moral condemnation, or worse, evils which of themselves *demand* the moralistic attitude. But is it so? Psychologically, moralism is "catching," at least in our society; to resist looks like a confession of indifference or complicity. How many can resist the sermons continually preached by Noam Chomsky, Susan Sontag, Dr. Spock, Mary McCarthy, and other well-known political sages in the *New York Review of Books*? Or, if that seems too easy, the earnest undergraduates, who two years ago weren't even reading the newspapers? And then there is always one's professional association, where year after year, one finds revolutionary advice offered to all, but chiefly to the President on such matters as war and peace, strategy, and various suggestions to who knows whom, deploring a variety of deplorable things, always of course in the name of morality and professional competence. Well, this too can be resisted.

But the question remains why a whole generation has chosen to sicken itself, to alienate itself from the one life granted it to live, and to render itself inefficacious for any genuine solution to genuine problems. Since that from which it has chosen to alienate itself is society as a whole, the Establishment, and even History, its alienation is in effect metaphysical, and not to disappear with the disappearance of any specific problem, such as the Vietnam war, the poverty pocket of Appalachia, or pollution from automobile exhaust. These then are not causes but occasions for the ignition of the passions in question, and when they fade away, there would be no reason in the world why others could not be found. The objects toward which passions direct themselves are not the causes of those passions; passions are responses of persons to objects, and the source of the passion is only to be found in the free choice of the man choosing to respond in that particular way. The present generation and its friends have chosen to adopt the attitude of moral distress; their only solace in their continual frustration seems to be a final extinction of personal responsibility, sinking into the Movement, where all swing and sway together, and no one is personally responsible since a Movement is nobody and turns all its members into nobodies. After the Movement, the communes; and, hopefully, after the communes a return to the family and society that once seemed so wicked and hateful, and then the bitter or amused memories of what it all was: an empty possibility, chosen perhaps simply because it was possible, new, groovy, and exciting, masking itself as moral and leaving behind not a trace of permanent value. It is already beginning to pall; and it was good that so much was written about it; posterity otherwise would not have been able to believe that so many otherwise intelligent people of good will could have said so many foolish or wicked things, actually believed them for a time, or that its more pathological devotees could have actually so ruined their own and others' lives by living these nightmares. Intellectually speaking, it is nothing but a repetition of some chapters of Hegel's *Phenomenology of the Mind*, sometimes carried to paroxysm; existentially speaking, it left its tragedies and ruins, which are not repetitions of anything, but final.

It is hard indeed to find anything whatsoever endearing in these contemporary radical escapades, particularly when played by those old enough to know better. So long as it remains talk, more good-humored talk is all that is called for; when it passes into bombings, treason, and personal violence, good humor would be silly, and those innocent of the knowledge of the power and majesty of their society must, willy-nilly, be made to feel it. If imagination can be gloriously frivolous, existence is not.

For one who is not in the least a friend of the Movement or of radical ideals, there remains the somewhat sour pleasure of a minor alienation itself, that is, an alienation from those who have alienated themselves. And as a compensation, a responsibility possible only to those who join no movements, and find their own friends and kindred spirits here and there, individually, and also in other seemingly happier times. The radical movement and the radical spirit are the maddenings produced in susceptible minds by the abstract idea; against them stands the spirit that remains loyal to its society, not as it forever might be, but *as it is*, with its own internal motives for stability, change, and improvement. In the long run the dispute is over the precious: the abstract that never has or never will be, against what is, existing men and their existing society, which did not come into being in an instant, which is fragile, which is not to be dismantled by the unexperienced and fanatical, and which is the sole context for values of this life.

# Two

# Paradoxes
# of Private Conscience

### The Question

THOUGHT SEEMS to thrive on crises to such an extent that when it can find none it either falls asleep or invents one. But surely most of the time it need only open its eyes; if there has ever been a substantial portion of human history without its crises, when was it? In any event, we hardly have to invent a crisis in the present day; one stares us in the face and it is indeed a crisis of thought. I refer of course to the conflict some men experience between the demands of public law and those of their private consciences, to wit, whether to obey the law demanding their participation in the Vietnam war or their own consciences, which may find that law morally intolerable. I should like to look into this question *without* raising the additional question whether *I* find that war a just one. That specific question is neither the premise nor conclusion to this discussion. And I should like to look at the question from the point of view not of those who approve of the war but only of those who *disapprove* of it since only there can our question be posed. The question could still be raised even if no one at all actually raised it.

And again, the question raised here is the *moral* resolution to a moral conflict between public law and private conscience; it is not the question whether a dissenter can *in fact* dodge the penalties of law, or whether the law has in fact the power to compel obedience. The answers to those questions would leave the moral issue untouched. And so we shall confine ourselves to one problem: what is the moral resolution to the possible conflict between one man's conscience and the law?

This question is obviously not itself a purely legal question, for what is at issue is the moral authority of laws themselves of which I may disapprove; it would beg the question to invoke those laws once again in their own self-defense. Nor, I believe, is it purely a question of my own conscience; for it is also the question of the absolute right of my own conscience against the laws which is raised. The laws give me no such legal right. If I begin by assuming the absolute authority of my own conscience, then I have also instantly come to the end of the problem and need only reiterate my principle at the conclusion. Neither simple answer is sensitive to the problematic character of the problem.

The problem is, of course, an ancient and recurring one; one need only recall the differing answers of Socrates and Aristotle, Galileo and Bruno, Thoreau and Emerson. My own little discussion will try to trace out dialectically and not historically the conflicting claims of private conscience and public law when each is taken by itself, put these claims into a dialogue, and then see what the conclusion might be, if there can be a conclusion.

### What Conscience Says

First, a few phenomenological remarks about what conscience is—"phenomenological" in the sense that these remarks only propose to discuss conscience *as it looks to itself,* not as it might look to a psychoanalyst, sociologist, historian, biologist, or to the faithful of any religion. Whatever else it might be, it primarily is a sense of right and wrong, of scruple that such a man without conscience, if one could be found, would regard himself as unscrupulous. Let us for the moment ignore the various things that men have regarded as right and wrong; we shall return to this later. But now we are looking at conscience itself no matter what moral language it speaks. And the first curious thing about it is that its *primary* word is "NO."

Conscience is most itself when it forbids some action, to such an extent that a "good conscience" approving my decisions looks far more like a case of self-satisfaction, self-righteousness, and moral smugness, which themselves could only be *disapproved* by my own conscience. Socrates' "daimon" only said "no."

Second, the primary address of my conscience is to me. It forbids *me* from doing certain things. Hence it is universally regarded as the very personal center of a man, his "inwit," as Middle English called it. It is the very person of the man and not some accidental or casual mental talent like a long memory or a lively imagination. It is so very much myself speaking to myself that radical conscientious self-criticism can tear the self apart. My violation of my own conscience then is hardly the same matter as making a mistake in arithmetic or miscalculating the practical effects of my decision. A violation of one's own conscience is hardly a "mistake" at all; it is more like the threat of dissolution of one's own deepest self.

And so, third, it is not difficult to understand why conscience always speaks with final authority for each. Sometimes it does not know whether to speak or not, the situation may be too obscure; or it may speak hypothetically, falteringly, and without blowing its certain note. But when it is most itself, it speaks with an unquestioned authority; do I indeed have anything higher than my own conscience to consult? But that could only be something my own conscience might reject. The authority with which conscience speaks when it does speak is so absolute that many men suppose it to be the voice of God, disobedience to which might carry with it eternal damnation.

The fourth note of conscience is that in its purity as a final authority for each man it is completely *abstract*. The conscience with which each man is born is nothing but a *sense* of right and wrong; it is not also already provided with the facts and the interpretation of facts necessary for its own exercise. If conscience then seems infallible, it is only because we are taking it in its abstract purity. So if the difference between right and wrong seems like a clear light, it is so only because it has not yet been turned on the ambiguities of the concrete domain where we must decide and act.

Now let us trace the course of the man of conscience in public affairs. Fortunately we do not have to invent, since Thoreau has already stated the matter with perfect clarity in his essay on civil disobedience, an essay which, supplemented by the works of Herbert Marcuse, has already taken on the authority of a higher Bible with the New Left, and in any event an authority far transcending that of the Constitution and the government together.

Thoreau puts the matter quite simply and plainly. He begins: "That government is best which governs least, or rather not at all." It is nothing but an "expediency" by which people exercise their will. And if this suggests a democracy, we are quickly disillusioned: "A government of majority rule in all cases can not be based on justice . . . can there not be a government in which not majorities decide right and wrong but conscience?" He then asks: "Must the citizen ever resign his conscience to the legislator?" The answer comes immediately: "The only obligation which I have a right to assume is to do at any time what I think right. . . . A wise man will not leave the right to the mercy of chance nor wish it to prevail through the power of the majority." How does conscience react to laws when it regards them as unjust? "All men recognize the right of revolution: to refuse allegiance to, to resist the government when its tyranny or its inefficiency are great and unendurable. . . . If injustice is such that it requires you to be the agent of injustice to another, then, I say, break the law." "Breaking the law," he specifies, means "using your whole influence," which includes one's life. He has nothing but scorn for those who merely use the ballot.

As for alternatives, he says: "Unjust laws exist; shall we be content to obey them, or shall we amend them and obey until we have succeeded, or shall we transgress at once?" But to obey them of course is to connive with evil; as for amendment, that, he says, "takes too much time and man's life will soon be gone." Besides, he adds, "I do not care to trace the course of my dollar. . . . It is for no particular item in the tax bill that I refuse to pay it. I simply wish to refuse allegiance to the State, to withdraw and stand aloof from it effectually." He ends: "Authority of government to be strictly pure must have the sanction and consent of the governed. It can have no right over my person and property but what I concede to it . . . the State must come to recognize the individual as a higher and independent power from which all its own power and authority are derived . . . and must treat him accordingly." As for his fellow citizens—those who obey the law because it is the law—they serve the state, he says, not as men mainly but as machines, with their bodies; they are, he adds, of the "same worth as horses and dogs." When he emerged from his night in jail, he had a new vision of his fellow townsmen; they now seemed to him to be of a "distinct race."

No doubt not all of this is strictly relevant to our present question, but it does offer the dialectical unfolding of an intransigent conscience confronting the claims of law. And, as must be obvious, its traditional name is anarchy, the withdrawal of allegiance from government and law in favor of the final accreditation by each man of his own solitary and ultimate conscience. Can any man of conscience do otherwise?

### What Laws Command

If this were the whole story, there would hardly be any problem at all. But it turns out to be *only* the voice of private conscience opposing its intimate and final claims to *other* claims, namely, those of the government and its laws. What might they say on their own behalf? If Thoreau says they derive their only authority from the approval of his private conscience, perhaps the most striking feature of the law is that it makes no mention whatsoever of Henry David Thoreau or any other private citizen as authenticating them. Is this an oversight?

If we now shift our point of view to that of government and its laws, what claims may they advance on their own behalf? But let us make a distinction between two sorts of law; there are, first of all, the ordinary, everyday enactments of an existing government. And, second, there is law of a different sort, those laws such as the Constitution of the United States which define the government itself and its legal powers. Everyday laws of the first sort somehow never mention

Thoreau or any other private citizen as giving them their authority; they claim authority from the government that enacts them. They lose authority if improperly passed or if in conflict with superior law, but never simply by virtue of being in conflict with Thoreau's conscience. Thoreau's conscience is then, from their point of view, strictly irrelevant to their authority. They are therefore morally or legally compelling upon Thoreau, whether he likes them or not. And to repeat, our question does not concern the obvious fact that the laws and their legal enforcement can *in fact* compel private obedience; it is whether they had any *right* to do so. If they derive their authority from the government and not from Thoreau, Thoreau can hardly represent his own conscience as their sole authorization, even for himself. And on top of this, it is the government which has the *moral* obligation to *enforce* its own laws; it is commonly recognized that laws that are not even capable of being enforced are but scraps of paper and not proper laws at all. But since Thoreau in his private person hardly has the means, let alone the right, to enforce those particular laws of his choice, by what authority can his private conscience claim to be the legislator of the world? In fact, the laws might continue (in this hostile vein), what initially looked like a beautiful appeal to conscience, on analysis, turns out to be the moral tyranny of *one* conscience over others and over the very government that it set up to adjudicate such problems.

Pursuing this last point, the laws might add the following. One would have to be very naive indeed to suppose that all consciences agree. If each man's conscience speaks with final and absolute authority, what it is speaking about is concrete decision and action. Now on conscience's own terms, one must conscientiously inform oneself of the very facts of the case being decided. No doubt in many cases these are sufficiently clear and agreed upon to offer no substantial problems; but surely not in all. A recent example might be the case of the *Pueblo*; another, the possibility of unidentified assassins of President Kennedy. On top of the difficulties of ascertaining the facts, there is a deeper one of *interpreting* or *reading* those facts. The very same facts can be put together in diverse ways, suggesting diverse judgments about them. In the Vietnam war, surely most of the dispute arises from this very source; if the question is whether the United States is there upon invitation of South Vietnam to prevent its invasion by North Vietnam and the Viet Cong, or whether we are invaders in a territory to which Ho Chi Minh can lay rightful claim, who could pretend that this is a simple factual question? Is the dispute clearly a case of reading the facts very differently, such that, at this date, no new *facts* will clinch the decision? On top of these sources of difference in conscientious decision, there is the final existential truth that my conscience is rooted in and expressive of *my own* deepest commitments; but so is the other man's. With the ambiguity of fact, the differences of reading those facts, and the final individuality of my concretely deciding conscience itself, it is hardly surprising that nothing is commoner than conflicts of conscience, not merely of one man with another, but of the same man with himself. Now if my conflicts with myself are strictly my own business, my conflicts with others are not; at this point I properly fall into the social and legal domain.

Now what can Thoreau do, armed only with the final authority of his own conscience, but declare one who disagrees with him lacking in conscience, or stupid or malicious, definitely a *lower* being; Thoreau saw them all as machines, dogs, and horses, a "different race." And with this particular species of moral fanaticism, surely the very atmosphere in which there might be a conscientious resolution to differences of conscience disappears. On the other hand, the laws might continue to argue, why were we, the laws, set up in the first place if not precisely to give a moral solution to moral conflicts? It is not a case of conscience versus the law but merely private conscience versus public conscience. Private must cede to public conscience.

Which brings us back to that more basic law, that which founds and authorizes government in the first place—in our case, the Constitution. Thoreau declared the Constitution to be not even worth thinking about from his higher point of view; and indeed why should it be when he has his private conscience to replace it? But perhaps the Constitution has something to say for itself. Since it supplies a primary justification for all consequent laws and authority, it can hardly be nothing. And yet in the ultimate probe, the founding law of any government is in what looks like a circle of justification. It is itself the authority for the government it sets up to uphold it. And so it is the authority for the authority of the very government it set up to enforce its authority. Here we have the possibility of a crisis in authority which becomes decisive in revolution.

And so chasing down final authority, now on the side of law and government, we may begin to see its own Achilles' heel. The highest law, the Constitution, was itself the act of men at the Constitutional Convention operating not under the Constitution but under other agreements which were to be superseded by the Constitution. What moral right did such men have to bind us in the future? And here it is of no avail to say that there are provisions in the Constitution for its own alteration; the procedures of alteration themselves must be constitutional or not; and so we are bound in the end *by* the Constitution *to* itself. Further, not all governments and founding laws have arisen this way; some just grew up through practice, tradition, and custom. Surely a large portion of what passes for legal decision even in a law-ridden country such as ours is and should be justified by custom, tradition, tacit understandings, and the rest. In a word, both *final* authority in law and government as well as a good deal of day-to-day rulings rest not upon law or government but custom, which, looked at from the point of view of law, is unformulizable, notoriously subject to differences of interpretation, and even changeable with the personalities of the administrators. If law and authority then can be said to be reasonable, that reasonability is itself ultimately founded on the irrational, historical, even the arbitrary.

If Thoreau then elevates his own conscience to an authority higher than government and law and thereby ironically turns into a private moral tyrant, the opposite claim of government, seeking to stabilize and adjudicate private disputes by an authority higher than individual consciences, finally passes from an initial rationality to a nonlegal, arbitrary, and irrational basis in historical acts, customs, tradition, and mere *de facto* practice.

### Can There Be a Resolution?

I have tried to take two claims for ultimate moral authority seriously, and run both into the ground. Neither, all by itself, can sustain its claim to *moral ultimacy*. If some such thing is true, what is to be done about it? Perhaps admit a little bit of both? But so far as I can see, there is no *theoretical* resolution to the problem whatsoever; and if this sounds disastrous, I should finally like to point out why I think it is, on the contrary, of utmost value and importance.

Thoreau himself was a gentle man, and so his principle of private conscience might seem a good deal more acceptable than it would if we were to compare two recent cases where violent men could appeal to the same principle. Both Lee Harvey Oswald and Sirhan Sirhan also used their consciences as their final guide, one to assassinate President Kennedy for his part in the Cuban crisis, the other to assassinate Senator Kennedy for his recommendations of aid to Israel. The reply that Thoreau was gentle and the latter two pathological only points up the limits of private conscience as a political guide. All could justify their conduct by their private consciences, but on the other hand there is the case of Colonel von Stauffenberg, who, at least in my own judgment, very nobly tried with some associates to assassinate Hitler. All were cases of conscience at its extremity in conflict with officers of the government if not the government itself. In some cases we may approve, in others, disapprove, but all would be equally authorized by the general principle of private conscience and all equally condemned by government and law. Can these cases now be judged either by law or by private conscience? Their own private consciences approved them; the law condemns them all, yet surely there are decisive differences among them.

On the other side, law is in the same boat. Law and government must have some prima facie justification up to a point; but revolution raises precisely that point. Law itself can hardly be taken as its own final justification. And yet no government and no law could possibly authorize each private citizen to pick and choose which laws he will obey and when and under what circumstances. Nor can any government regard itself as anything but the legal government; those who refuse to recognize its *moral* authority are not citizens of that country but in effect potential enemies of the State. And yet who would not have to recognize the possibility of a radically corrupt state, corrupt not in its own terms but in terms drawn from other sources, perhaps even finally private conscience?

I believe these paradoxes to be *theoretically insoluble*, that is, that there can be *no general principle* or method that we could consult to prove in all extremities which side must be right, which wrong. And, far from being an intellectual disaster, on the contrary it throws into relief some existential points. First of all, if we *could* solve these paradoxes theoretically, once and for all, while we might take some thin pleasure in the fact, we would at the same stroke have removed all sense whatsoever from the historical struggles of men, from existence itself. Installing ourselves in the divine seat of judgment, either of private conscience or law, we would be entitled to pronounce on the past and future course of history and would in effect be viewing it as a senseless struggle of either stupid or immoral men with wise and moral men who always more or less are pictured in our own image. Having solved in this chapter the problem of existence, *it* could have nothing further to teach us. Second, if any such attempted vision eliminates the essential moral *risk* of existence, it also prepares the atmosphere for that pseudodiscussion where neither side listens but each only speaks out of private moral or public legal certitudes. Conscience slips into fanaticism and criminality, becoming an enemy of the State; government and law can become enemies of the very conscience that defines each man. To ask for general criteria and standards is to ask for not merely what is impossible but, I am convinced also, precisely that which would obfuscate the problem by declaring it solved for life.

Meanwhile there are some interesting examples of the ultimately *insoluble* character of the conflict. Socrates, condemned by the law, declared he would not harm the laws themselves and drank the hemlock. Aristotle, also condemned on similar laws, declared he would not permit Athens to sin twice against philosophy and retired to a country estate. Bruno, condemned for his metaphysics and astronomy, went to the stake for them; Galileo recanted, adding, however, that he was still right. Thoreau went to jail for a night, an act incomprehensible to Emerson, who bailed him out. And so the examples multiply. My inclination is not to pronounce judgment on these cases, but to point to the irreducible paradoxes of *both* law *and* private conscience as final guides to anything; to retain the paradox is to restore to our sense of existence its own paradoxicality and risk, where at last there can be nothing but listening and acting. And after decision, even here, there are no final *guarantees* that any choice ever was right or wrong. To sum up briefly: I have tried to present something like an exposition of the dialectic of listening. Listening, if it were nothing but a receptivity to diversity of opinions, could easily lead to paralysis of will. And, after having heard the possible options laid before me, I *still* have to decide; the options before me won't decide of themselves. And further, any decision whatsoever involves two matters: the course of action itself and the principle by which I justify that choice or authorize it to and for myself. My own discussion has involved this last factor, that by which I ultimately justify my political choices.

At first, the ultimate judge and moral authority looks simple: it is my own conscience. Here we met Thoreau. And we continue to meet his descendants in all those who without more ado simply bring each choice before their private consciences and rule upon that choice with a frightening finality.

But, second, if conscience is conscientious enough, it will look into itself: what is it but an abstract sense of right and wrong, clear because empty of any particular information? And so a conscientious examination of conscience discloses that it has some unique disqualifications to rule on the world. As soon as it judges any particular matter of fact, it has descended into a domain where it loses its abstract majesty and looks like one more party to the quarrel, with incomplete information, faced with a diversity of equally plausible readings of what information it has, and finally resolving the whole thing by a pronouncement that inevitably reflects the personal situation and biases of the person whose conscience it is. It is but one conscience among many.

Having a sentiment of this from the beginning, men have taken the next step: set up a public conscience, law, whose sole justification is to settle, by an agreed upon ethical procedure, differences among private consciences. At this stage of the dialectic, private conscience, which remains conscientious and not a blind fist of power masquerading as moral, must cede to that moral authority, the law, which it set up in the first place to resolve these differences. At this stage of listening, the law has a moral authority transcending any private conscience.

A third stage emerges when the man of private conscience, having gone through the prior stages and not before, finds the very foundations of the law under which he has consented to live incompatible with his conscience. At this point, he has chosen to be outside the law, cannot reasonably expect its protection, and takes upon himself, in both his conscience and his own particularity as a finite historical man, the authorization and justification of his own social acts. In effect he has become his own lawgiver or, following Nietzsche, is beyond good and evil. If such a man rejects the principle of law as such, he is simply an anarchist and has reverted to stage one, each for himself. If he does not reject the principle of law but only a particular set of laws, wishing to replace them with others, then let him find his followers and let them collectively judge whether they now have something better or worse, or just different.

In all of this there is hardly any logical or purely rational solution. The last stage is the stage of revolution; there are no *abstract* principles by which to judge the worth of revolution. And as for *particular* principles, it is exactly they which are being revolved. At this point the revolutionary is strictly and eternally on his own; right and wrong in the domain of action do not have the meaning of logically correct or incorrect. They refer to values, and the sole authority values possess is their ability to engage our deepest will. They are neither correct nor incorrect, but affirmed or rejected. This dialectic of listening has sought only to indicate some stages of questioning that must be engaged in so that the deepest affirmation will indeed proceed from our existence and not some chance rage of the moment.

# Three

◇◇◇

# *Myself as Moral Hero*

It is not my intention to try Daniel Ellsberg *in absentia.* Still, what we can presume to be the facts of the case, admitted by Ellsberg in public, supply us with more than enough material for thought. In a moment we shall have left Ellsberg personally anyway; his case is but one in a long history of men who violate the laws of their country in the name of a "higher value" perceived by their private conscience.

The brief facts are well known and seem to be these: Mr. Ellsberg finally after much consideration convinced himself that his nation was fighting an unjust war. He then came to know of certain secret documents which, he felt, would inform the public of how we came to embark on that war. With that knowledge, the public would agree with him on the injustice of the war. His conscience would not permit him to keep silent on what he knew; the law ordered silence. He decided to break the law, reveal the contents of the Pentagon papers. The charge is guilty of breaking the law; his plea is "innocent." Whether this is the case or not, let us stipulate it for discussion.

In all of this, much of the internal drama, perhaps its most interesting side, will have to be omitted. It unquestionably would be superb material for a novelist, a Conrad, Melville, or Dostoievsky. Our own purpose is different and more humble: by schematizing the problem and reflecting upon the prima facie dilemma, perhaps to learn a little more deeply some lessons valid even for less dramatic cases, in everyday life.

In order to reflect upon this matter, certain attendant

questions must be put within brackets. And perhaps the first of them are the passions we feel for or against that war. The question of the justice of the war itself will return; but only after its pertinence has been established. Nor are our sympathies or antipathies for Mr. Ellsberg of the slightest pertinence. Those could only be justified after a scrutiny of his conduct. Nor are we particularly interested in the value or lack of value of the Pentagon papers themselves; for some they were a "revelation"; for others, trivialities, more or less known or at least suspected; for still others, disclosures of no relevance whatsoever to the issue of the war itself. All these reactions would be exceedingly difficult to assess, and for the question I would like to elicit, irrelevant. The truth is, no doubt, after their full disclosure very few indeed have had the time or inclination to read them through. Still, that is hardly Ellsberg's fault.

In the first and perhaps last instance, it is hard indeed to see our stipulated Ellsberg as anything but guilty. In fact, the Ellsberg problem would not be a problem except by granting his prima facie guilt. If he were indeed innocent of breaking the law, precisely what was his conscience wrestling with? Has he not admitted that the papers were not merely classified, but known by him to be classified? Is anything more needed for a simple verdict of guilt? That the evidence was improperly gathered and the charges subsequently withdrawn hardly affects our problem at all. We need only rerun the trial in our imagination where the evidence would be collected legally, the law itself clear, and the prosecution's case made without fault. And the same is true of the proprieties of his defense; if they were to be faulty, no matter; the philosophical problem of Ellsberg and his countless likenesses through history are not touched by the facts of the matter, nor the actual progress of the case.

Let us in addition imagine that the Pentagon papers contained disclosures of the highest interest: official lying or misrepresentation, in a word, matter implicating members of the government itself in crime, as Ellsberg himself must believe, facts which if known would persuade many citizens to condemn the policy of the government as well as those members responsible for it. In short, let us suppose for the argument that matters are pretty much as Ellsberg supposes; after all, that was the moral scene in which he acted and which suggests the problem.

The problem can, I think, be simply stated: what are we to think of a man who himself is tempted to violate a law in order to disclose what he thinks is the violation of a "higher law" by the government? This, it seems, was the dilemma facing Ellsberg, one in which he resolved to act as he did. His conscience *compelled* him; and in the long run, that could be his only defense. Our problem then is to scrutinize *conscience as a defense for illegal action*.

Theoretically, neither the laws themselves nor the government enforcing them can tolerate private conscience as a defense for violating laws. No law could be written that would simultaneously grant any citizen the right to exempt himself from its jurisdiction when his private conscience permitted. Clearly, such laws would be self-nullifying. The Chicago police were unimpressed, therefore, when a few years back some speeding Jehovah's Witnesses exempted themselves from the traffic code on the grounds that the Old Testament contained no such provisions, which must therefore have proceeded from nothing but men whose rule they did not admit; were they to be slowed down in their zeal to attend a meeting with God by mere men?

That the laws do not allow their own violation, does not, of course, prevent judges from exercising *mercy*, the remission of a punishment legally earned. But mercy is not formalizable into law without the nullification of the law itself; if mercy is to be granted always and everywhere under specifiable conditions, then what mercy sought to accomplish should be written into the law itself. Mercy presupposes guilt and does not remove it; it merely suspends punishment.

If private conscience is no defense against the violation of law, simply because the law does not permit *any* defense against itself, there are yet other reasons that make the inviolability of law plausible. In the first instance, the law regards itself as *public* conscience, the just resolution publicly of a multitude of private consciences, all claiming different things. It cannot look upon itself therefore as a mere convenience, or mere power without moral justification. It is what the public at any time has resolved to be the moral code for itself. It is therefore public *morals*, not a sheer fact of power; and what opposes the moral claim of *public* conscience is not conscience itself; it is nothing but *private* conscience. But indeed to be a citizen is to recognize the authority of the public conscience over my own private conscience. To repeat, this authority is a *moral* authority, and has nothing to do with the public force that may be brought to bear to ensure enforcement. To look upon the clash of private conscience with law as that of conscience with public *power* is to seriously misunderstand the moral authority of law itself.

Next, the assumption that conscience in its private exercise is manifested only when it violates the law is to make the frightful implication that those who do not violate the law are acting without conscience. Hence "conscientious action" invariably carries the connotation that law-abiding citizens are acting without conscience, a conclusion dear to Henry Thoreau, but one that is the same as moral arrogance.

It is not hard to see that common courtesy and common respect for one's fellow citizens must assume that all men act conscientiously, not merely those who conspicuously violate law. That all men *in fact* do not act conscientiously has nothing to do with the matter.

And finally, if conscience is to be a defense of illegal action, there is the consequence that all trials of the accused must become inquiries or inquisitions into their consciences. Did they or did they not act according to their consciences? Is the heat of their words sufficient proof? Their past record? Their lack of any other obvious motive? Does the accused himself know that he acted in accordance with his conscience? Was his conscience morbid or diseased? The prospect of a frightful and interminable psychoanalysis opens up, now with psychologists becoming decisive judges. And at this point, has not the legitimate claim of law been altogether forgotten?

In sum does the consideration of "conscience" really add anything that a court of law must take into consideration in determining guilt? It would of course be pertinent to any mercy the judge might choose to exercise. But then the *plea* of private conscience looks more and more like a plea for mercy on grounds of not being in one's right mind. The thorny thing about conscience, however, is that it insists unto the end that it *is* the right mind of the guilty; which means the guilty is unrepentant, a fact in itself that would not encourage mercy. At this point one reaches the dialectic of fanaticism.

Purely considered, conscience is nothing but the *form* of moral judgment. By itself it can say nothing but that this is good or that bad; in fact, in its absolute purity it is not entitled to the "this" or "that," which represent dubitable choices in existence, dependent on fallible data and interpretation. It therefore is nothing but the *formal* consciousness of good or bad. But the forms of good and bad have to be applied to this or that in order to dictate action. Now, unquestionably, good is good and bad is bad; and that is as absolute as possible and as empty of consequences as possible. Plato put the form of the Good into a timeless place of Pure Form or Being. Action, alas, occurs in another domain, that of existence or Becoming. And that's the rub. Conscience, so long as it is pure and inviolable, can make no decisions; as soon as it does, it enters into the domain of the problematic, relative, and dubitable, in short, precisely that domain which is susceptible to discussion, questioning, probabilities, compromises. In a word, it falls into the domain of politics with its debates, provisional resolutions, all based upon the conviction that the differences that separate men separate them as differently moral, not simply moral versus immoral. Conscience then, when sufficiently conscientious, reverts back to the public domain of law.

Now how, indeed, can private conscience, that of Mr. Ellsberg or anyone else, grant itself the privilege of abridging, correcting, or reversing this entire political process, to be defended by nothing stronger than that it *feels* so? Do we not all have consciences; has not our collective resolution been incorporated into law? Would Mr. Ellsberg wish a system in which anyone could violate the laws of classification of documents at will? Has he not then, in effect, no matter what his personal humility may or may not be, claimed a divine right he would not grant to all, if any other? Does not anyone who violates the law on grounds of conscience claim some such divine right for himself? And is not this the essential fanaticism of private conscience? As a consequence we see essential absurdities in any legal defense of a criminal through the argument that he was "conscientious."

And yet. The public conscience, expressed in its positive laws, and enforced by the administration behind those laws, is itself finite. It is a provisional codification of what men at a given time think just and expeditious. But if a single, private citizen is indeed finite in both his sense of justice as well as his reading of the factual scene where that conscience must operate, so too is a society. No one who has considered some of the more patently frightful governments, with their "laws," could possibly decide otherwise. And for this purpose it makes no difference whatsoever whether the laws are imposed by a totalitarian dictatorship or by democratic approval; a *demos* can be as deluded and fanatic as a dictator. In any event they are both finite, determinate, and no matter how well- or ill-intentioned, merely *one* sense of an infinite ideal. In their own terms, no doubt both the Hitlerian and the Stalinist governments were legal, and possessed the full authority implicit in legality. If therefore one judges these systems profoundly bad, one is not doing it through an analysis of their own internal values and rules. Some other ideal is brought to bear from outside such systems. From where then except that private conscience which distinguishes itself from legal authority? At which point, private conscience appears as a source of a fresh morality, not incorporated within the existing system, and *perhaps* higher. But *if* it is higher, it is not higher in legal authority. In what terms then? Obviously, in that pure ideal, that pure form of the Good, which conscience, or the moral sense, envisages, and in the light of which it criticizes existing law or practice. It envisages something better than what is. That pure form of the Good is most frequently called God, but then the name hardly matters; the atheist anarchists of the Spanish Civil War called it Justice, or something else.

There is, then, and always will be the occasion for such a dispute between my own conscience and that of the public on some specific law, though not law as such. And what a feeble thing my own conscience is when confronted with practical action, with its indefinite consequences, innumerable considerations, and with the fallible information upon which it must decide on the one hand, and on the other the massive authority of law and government, that very government we set up in the first place precisely to relieve private conscience of such decisions, to ascertain facts, consequences of decisions, to read the whole public scene in which decisions have force and consequences.

If we have ended in an unsatisfactory dilemma, that which gives right to *both* sides of an implacable quarrel, at least a few things have been settled: the law *can* and *should* do nothing but punish its violators. Further, the conscientious violator himself, insofar as he is a citizen, has already implicitly consented to his own punishment. The plea of innocence then is absurd. Innocent of what?

And yet, who could deny that *some* such violators are indeed benefactors of all? Count von Stauffenberg organized an unsuccessful attempt to assassinate Hitler. The list of such heroes could be extended, but then something becomes questionable: are all conscientious attempts to assassinate heads of government to be approved? There was Lee Harvey Oswald, who assassinated President Kennedy on grounds of a political, i.e., conscientious opposition to his Cuban affair. There was Sirhan Sirhan, who also consulted his conscience to determine that Robert Kennedy must die for his sympathy with Israel. Now then, *how are we to decide*, among all the cases in history of the conflicts between private and public conscience, which are *really* right and which wrong?

The question "how are we to decide who is really right—the law or private conscience?" raises two final points: (1) it asks for a "how," namely a rule for deciding; and (2) it has in mind what is "really right." With regard to the perpetual search for rules, as sensible as that might seem to computer programmers, it is obvious on the face of it that not everything is determinable by rule; and one of the most conspicuous of these cases is precisely *when* the rule must be opposed. If, therefore, private conscience decides of itself to violate the rule of law, there can be no additional rule it can consult. It is strictly beyond rule, and it is that which it decides; but that decision is not and cannot itself be brought under further rules. Such situations were deeply studied by Kierkegaard in *Fear and Trembling* and elsewhere. To locate oneself beyond justification by rule, which is where private conscience is located in its opposition to law, is to be where singular human existence is at those limits Karl Jaspers calls boundary situations *(Grenzsituationen)*. At these limits *I* must take personal responsibility for my violation of the rule. Taking responsibility means the assumption of my guilt, and not an attempt to obfuscate the matter so that I now look innocent. My only plea could be for mercy. And on what grounds could mercy be extended; again, no rule for that either, but the residual perception that existing laws are finite, though they must claim unconditional obedience.

With regard to the second point above, namely that violation of the law is permitted when the violator is *really right,* the truth is that the notion of *really* being right is wholly vacuous in the present context. Between the individual and his society all that is present is a clash of *views* of the right, not that really Right itself which Plato assigned to the pure realm of Form. And since the dispute is precisely over who *is* really right, or who has the most unclouded view of it, that absolute Right itself hovering over the dispute is not a party to it. On the face of it, law itself in its capacity of being law is the moral determiner of factual right; the violator is a criminal and must suffer the consequences. That he may have felt himself to be really right may be interesting for his psychology, but it hardly affects the fact of the crime, or the punishment it deserves.

All of which leaves room for approval of those whom the law must regard as criminal but whom posterity may thank for whatever effect the crime had in improving some state of affairs. It could never thank anyone for weakening law as such; but it might for other consequences. Formally, there can be no rule for deciding in general between legal criminals we would praise and those we curse. Both may have "consulted their consciences." Both must be declared guilty; and suffer their punishment. And yet some we must praise as heroes.

If this ultimate paradox seems unsatisfactory, on the other

hand, to sustain it is to sustain also the essential meaning and freshness of human existence. It is some such thing that life is about, which gives a creative value to both history and individual human life they would not have if either rule or absence of rule were alone to exist. Life is not itself exhaustively subsumable under rule or method although rule is an essential component. In a word, is not human existence, when authentic, always having to decide precisely such matters? And if so, then it would be no service to imagine the whole affair either solely determinable by rule or, on the other hand, without rule at all, or to look for the final rule to settle when either should prevail.

# Four

◇◇◇

# In Defense of War

A PHILOSOPHICAL CONSIDERATION of political affairs has the disadvantage of being incapable, in and of itself, of implying any specific practical action or policy. It would, then, seem useless except for the accompanying reflection that specific policy undertaken without any attention to principles is mindless; and mindless action can have no expectation either of practical effect or of intellectual defense. No doubt the relation of principles to action is complex indeed; but at least it can be said that practical principles without reference to possible action are vacuous, and action that cannot be clarified by principle is aimless commotion. Principled action offers us, then, the best that can be hoped for. That, however, is the work not of philosophy but of statesmanship, a faculty which is as theoretically clear as it need be but also skilled by experience in reading the existing political scene. Accordingly my present remarks aim only at some principles involved in the understanding of war, focusing on those that seem conspicuously absent in contemporary discussion, and not at defending any specific judgments about the Vietnam war. Examples of incoherent principles will be drawn from recent discussions; but any other war might have served equally well. No judgment about that particular can be derived from these remarks on principles; and if most of the false principles are quoted from the antiwar side, it is only because that side has been more vocal.

The villain of the present essay is *pacifism,* by which I mean a principled opposition to all war. Since it is a principled opposition, any appropriate opposition to pacifism must itself be a matter of principles. That pacifism is a principle and not a specific opposition to this war is sufficiently indicated by the suffix "ism," as well as by the arguments it mounts to make its principle plausible: it is war itself that is evil, and peace itself good, under no matter what terms. Pacifists think it is enough to declare these ideals to win all hearts and minds; and if to some people these pacifist principles seem impractical or indeed immoral, that can only be because the unconverted are hard of heart, slow of comprehension, or the world itself not yet ready for such a glory. That pacifism itself is practically absurd and morally deplorable is the chief burden of my remarks. The argument will be by way of excavating the presuppositions and tracing the consequences of pacifism, and exhibiting them to the reader for his free choice. That pacifism itself is evil does *not*, needless to say, imply that the *persons* who hold that view are evil; a radical distinction between the character of persons and the character of their articulated views is the very basis of this or any other civilized discussion. If human beings could not be decent while their views are absurd, then all of us would fall into the abyss.

In any event, the first casualty of the Vietnam war seems to have been philosophy itself. The transition was easy: from an opposition to the war on whatever ground, a portion of the public mind rose to what it thought was the proper principle of that opposition: pacifism, the sentiment that war was itself evil. And its arguments proceeded down from that height. Flattering themselves for their "idealism," pacifists could only survey the home reality they had left with high indignation: we were killing! Children were trotted forth on TV to ask: why must men kill one another? Can we not all love one another, the child asks, having immediately forgotten his fight with his brother off-screen. Having been illuminated by the purity and innocence of children, the new pacifist can but flagellate himself in public remorse. Not merely must this war be stopped at once, but all war and forever; we must recompense our enemies for the damage wrought upon them; we must ask their forgiveness, for are they not really our friends and our friends our enemies? And as the confusion multiplies and moral passion inflames itself, nothing appears as too severe a punishment for ourselves; impeachment of our leaders and finally the impeachment of ourselves and our history seem too gentle. These public outbursts of moral self-hatred are, of course, not unknown in history; let Savonarola stand for them all. Today the uproar is orchestrated by retired baby doctors, neurotic poets and novelists, psychoanalysts, ministers, and confused philosophers, each of whom, armed with the authority of his special "insight," seeks to speak for suffering humanity. The message to be read through the tear-stained faces is the same: we must stop killing! Regardless of how one reads the Vietnam war, what is *said* publicly for or most usually against it presents something like the eclipse of political thought. And with the eclipse of thought, we are left with some of the most preposterous slogans ever to find utterance. When supported by high passion, parades and demonstrations, insults in loud voices, we find ourselves once again in the theater of the absurd.

### Why War?

Why indeed, asks the child? Why cannot everyone love one another? Settle all disputes "rationally," so that all men could live as brothers, already having forgotten the first brothers, Cain and Abel? Thrashing around for explanations of the horrid fact that people can indeed be hostile to one another, the sloganeer with a smattering of popculture finds some answers ready to hand. War has a biological origin; it arises from an excess of testosterone in the male; maybe there is a biological solution, something like castration? That Indira Gandhi and Golda Meir have conducted their wars very successfully is already forgotten. Or maybe they are men in disguise? Or the impulse to fight arises from some distorted family history, a son conditioned by a father who in turn was conditioned by his father to conceive war as particularly masculine, an expression of *machismo;* but that could be remedied by "treatment." Perhaps drugs, suggested a recent president of the American Psychological Society. Or perhaps war arises from selfishness, a moral flaw that could be remedied by the sort of turn of the heart hoped for by a Quaker who during WW II looked Hitler straight in the eye and said: "Thou art an evil man!" If there is a warlike "instinct," maybe it could be diverted into harmless games like chess or the Olympics. And then maybe there is no such instinct? Animals may be found like the gazelle or lamb, which are not particularly aggressive; why not take them for our ideal? Or, if not an animal "instinct," then surely it is generated by the capitalist society, which, as everyone knows, fosters aggression, competition, acquisitiveness, and imperialism. But then even the most casual glance sees that Communist societies are even more imperialist and aggressive than capitalist. And does not the stock market fall with each new bombing? Or, finally, it is all caused by presidents, who wish to be mentioned in the history books, or be reelected by the V.F.W. The presidency should accordingly be abolished; policy should be turned over to the people. But which people? Those people who have been treated, have had a change of heart, who take flowers and gentle animals for their ideal, in a word, the remnant who through their dictatorship will save the world from every war except that against themselves.

The generating assumption of this system of explanations is of course that there can be no *moral justification* for war at all. It is simply an evil; and since man is "naturally good," one must look for a cause of his distorted conduct. If war were morally justifiable, then that justification would remove any occasion for looking for pathological explanations. If one does not seek causes for a man doing good works other than the goodness of the work itself, neither need one seek biological, psychological, cultural, sociopolitical causes for a justifiable war. The justification *is* the cause in this case.

And so then the question Why war? would be answered if any moral justification for it were forthcoming. A "justifiable war"? Is that not a contradiction in terms, or is it the pacifist who represents a living contradiction in terms?

This first answer to the question Why war? assumes at the start that it *is* evil, assumes that men are or could be "naturally good," meaning "peaceful," but since in point of fact they are not, the "explanation" is to be found in an artificial distortion of their passionate nature. The elimination of war will result from a correction of that passionate nature, through treatment, whether physiological, psychological, social, or rhetorical. Either their bodies or their characters must be changed by whatever treatment promises success. The lion will lie down with the lamb, indeed will be indistinguishable from him. He will abandon pride, greed, egotism, the desire to display power, to intimidate, to coerce; he will at the end of history at last be good. But, of course, absolutely *all* men must be good; for if even a few are left who do *not* so envisage the good, our "good" men will be, of course, good-for-nothing, and their peace will be the peace determined by the wicked. Unwilling to fight for their lives or ideals, they are suppressed and at that point the whole of human history recommences as if there had been no interlude, or at best an interlude within common sense. The lamb who lies down with the lion may indeed be good for the lion when his appetites return; and if he is good in any other sense, it could only be on a mystic plane not exactly pertinent to the practical moral plane of existence. It is not surprising, then, that advocates in the church of the kingdom of heaven do indeed place it in heaven, but never advocate it as political policy. After all, by definition heaven has already expelled or refused admittance to the wicked, hence is hardly faced with problems commensurate with ours on earth. What does a lion *eat* in heaven? Men, needless to say, are not animals *simpliciter,* but rational or spirited animals; but neither reasons nor spirit so long as they remain living can *contradict* animal needs.

That rational animals engage in hostilities unto death has always seemed a scandal to those philosophers who neglect existence. If one stamp of moralist finds both the cause and solution to war in some alteration in body or character, many philosophers of abstractions find both the cause and solution to war in thought, to be corrected by right reasoning. If rational men still fight, and if war is irrational, then there must be a rational solution to it. The medium of reason is the word, so we can expect this stamp of pacifist to praise the verbal solution to hostilities: the treaty. Would it not be reasonable to prevent or terminate hostilities by calculation, agreements, and solemnly pledged words? It is easy to forgive philosophers and the educated in general for their touching confidence in the power of words; they exercise a magical power in and over the mind; but perhaps that is their proper place. However, it is an outrageous neglect to fancy that they have any power except that over the mind, mind, moreover, which itself has the obligation to superintend the very existential conditions of its own life. Who then is surprised when he reads that in the last three hundred and fifty years, something like eighty-five percent of the treaties signed in the Western world have been broken? But the treaty theory of peace can then congratulate itself on the fact that now a culprit can be identified, declared to be an aggressor, and, while the aggressor is condemned by the "enlightened good will of mankind," he nevertheless proceeds to enjoy his dinner, and later may be celebrated as a benefactor of mankind; he will certainly not hesitate to sign new treaties. Our question is what to do: wring one's hands over men's irrationality or rethink the meaning of war? In all of this, one can easily agree that treaties exercise some slight restraining power over the more rapacious inclinations; but would it not be criminal neglect to entrust the security of one's country to treaties? And, in fact, does any responsible leader ever do it? No doubt, the lambs, since they have nothing better to work with.

And eventually, as the final rational solution to the problem of war, there is the idea of a single super state, whether an enlargement of one of those now extant—such as the U.S.A., Russia, or China—or conceived as a super United Nations. This convulsive, "final solution" to the war problem particularly appeals to those who have little "negative capability," as Keats put it, little tolerance for the uncertain, for risk, for in fact the most fundamental characteristics of free human life. When put in the form of a super United Nations, it almost looks harmless, mostly because its prototype, the present United Nations, is harmless. But it can more properly be put in uglier terms; if it were indeed to be a super state, it could be nothing short of a super totalitarianism. The historical totalitarianisms we have all witnessed would be as nothing compared with this monstrosity; and, as has often been remarked, they grew in precisely the same spiritual soil, a certain inability to face risk, death, war, or confusion, to face the existential conditions of a free life with dignity. Everything must be put *in order!* And if it is not now in order and never has been, then the order will be imposed, imposed in fact by that very Force which once seemed so odious. A new order of the World; but now its dissidents become World enemies and where are they to flee? Do they have a right to life itself? Are they not enemies of the World? In this abstract fantasia, the first thing lost sight of is a small annoying matter, a point of logic: any Order is also only itself a *specific* order. Law and Order, of course, are only universal abstractions, whose proper medium of existence is the word. In existence itself, it is always this or that order, that is, *somebody's* order; and then there is always somebody else who believes honestly in another order, one perhaps more favorable to himself or his ideal. Again the eternal hostilities break out, now, however, with a difference: hostilities between nations have not been eliminated, but only redubbed: each is now a *civil* war within the World State. Perhaps the candid observer will be excused if he fails to perceive the difference, except in the new savagery now morally permitted. And as for the individual? He has been forgotten for a long time in his prison or madhouse. He must be given therapy.

Many serious persons, of course, are sensitive to these paradoxes, and yet finally in desperation cling to the solution of a world state or world dictatorship as the only preventative of world destruction through nuclear holocaust. It is one thing to be willing to give one's own life for one's nation, but it is qualitatively different to destroy the habitable parts of the globe for "nothing but" freedom and dignity. For our present discussion we shall assume that some such thing is possible now or in the not too distant future. The possibility raises questions, obviously, of an ultimate order. But I do not think it unambiguously true that some such possible world catastrophe compels assent to world totalitarianism. In any event, for the moment, it might seem that here, at last, pacifism becomes sanity; and that any acceptance of world destruction is the very essence of evil and immorality. I shall revert to this question at the end and I touch upon it now only to complete this first part that surveys various sentiments which find war as such and in principle intolerable and which make efforts to formulate a solution or eliminate the cause.

## The Justification of War

The attitudes so far considered begin, as we have seen, by assuming war to be unjustifiable; *if* it is unjustifiable, then its cause must be found in biological, psychological, social, or moral distortions of an inherently peace-loving human nature; the cure is always some form of therapy. Or those who conduct war must have reasoned badly or given up the hope that rational discussion with its eventual treaty would be effective. Wars are "irrational," no philosophical justification of any is possible; thought will find the rational "solution." But on the other hand, if war is justifiable, then the search for its causes either in distortions of the passionate nature of man or in errors or failures of reason is downright foolish. The justification removes the premise of the search for causes and cures. The justification of war as a form of moral and rational excellence may seem scandalous to the pacifist, and yet it is that scandal I should like to defend. And as for talk about the greater or lesser of two evils, I shall try to avoid this ambiguous, slippery, and ultimately meaningless effort to calculate the incalculable. The justification of war aims at showing both its morality and its rationality; if, therefore, there are occasions when a moral and rational man must fight, then a proscription of war in principle must be itself irrational and ethically deplorable.

The justification of war is existence; to will to exist is to affirm war as its means and condition. But perhaps the term "existence" puts the matter too abstractly. In the present context, and in its most abstract sense, existence is a synonym for life, and nonexistence for death. Wars, then, are justified as means taken to assure life and death. And yet little has been said; the life and death of what? Bare life measured by the beating of the heart is hardly life at all; it would be prized only as the supporter and condition of a life worth living. Obviously men have always thought it justifiable to fight not merely to preserve their physical being, but also for those additional things that make that life worth living: fertile lands, access to the sea, minerals, a government of their choice, laws and customs and religions, and finally peace itself. Existence, then, is hardly bare survival but an existence in the service of all those concrete values which illuminate and glorify existence. They too must exist; it is almost by definition that values, in and of their intrinsic meaning, *demand existence.* Justice would misunderstand itself if it were content to remain abstract and merely ideal.

So much might easily be granted until another reflection arises, that perhaps the goods of existence could be shared by all men. This utopian notion is much beloved of *philosophers* and *art critics* who look upon the diversities of thought and cultural style as so many advantages and opportunities for spiritual growth. As indeed they are; but then those values are not exactly what war is about. If the library can house every book in peaceful coexistence, or if the museum can calmly exhibit the styles of the world, why must men themselves fight? Could the world not be like an international congress of philosophy or perhaps a quieter meeting of UNESCO: would this not be the civilized thing? Would it not be better if nations conducted themselves according to the model of a genteel conversation, where views are advanced and withdrawn without anger, and where men say "excuse me for interrupting"?

But elementary reflection is enough to dispel these dreams. Existence or life individuates itself; when it can speak, it says "I," and when it possesses, "mine." Nothing is changed logically in this respect when the I becomes a we, and the mine, ours. That I am not you, or we are not they, is the ineluctable ground of war; individuation is essential to existence. That which is not individuated does not exist, but subsists as a universal or abstract meaning. Consequently the meaning of a book or cultural artifact can be shared by all; but the existent book or existent painting cannot, and could supply a ground for conflict. No wonder philosophers or scientists or critics, accustomed to living in the domain of abstractions and ideal meanings that are not, like quantities of matter, diminished progressively by each man who partakes of them, find something scandalous and primitive about war or anything else appropriate in the domain of existence and life. Nothing is easier than for the spirit to neglect the conditions of its own existence, or indeed be outraged by them.

I have used the term "existential" intentionally in spite of its abstractness to avoid at all costs what might seem to be its more common equivalent, "material." Some sentimental pacifists think it sufficient to prove that a nation has gone to war for "material" interests to conclude, with cheers from their audience, that such a war is *immoral*. That idealism should find itself opposed to "matter," or its equivalent, life and existence, would certainly not have surprised the Buddha or Nietzsche, both of whom accurately perceived that the only surcease of war and public sorrow is in nothingness, Nirvana, or eternity. And, as President Truman remarked, those who cannot stand the heat should get out of the kitchen.

But, of course, what the sentimental pacifist wants is nothing so radical as the genuine alternative of a Buddha; he wants an existent heaven, perpetual peace-on-earth, a mishmash which has never been or never will be seen, violating as it does patent ontological differences subsisting between existence and the abstract. The exposure of this error is not difficult. At what precise point do material interests become ideal? Is the health of a nation "material" or "ideal"? But its health depends, of course, upon its wealth; is the pursuit of that wealth ideal or materialistic and crass? Is the culture of a nation an ideal or a material value? And is its culture dependent or not upon the wealth available for education and leisure? Is the wealth devoted to such tasks materialistic or idealistic? Money versus human life! All these false contrasts need not be multiplied to perceive the vacuity of any argument against war based upon "idealistic" as opposed to "materialistic" principles.

Functioning according to the same false logic is another simplistic contrast, also beloved of pacifists: that thought to exist between egoism and altruism. The high-minded rhetoric poured out against "selfishness" is laughable indeed when not taken seriously. Is it "selfish" for me to protect my own life, or those of my family, friends, or compatriots? And, moreover, not merely our physical existence, but our human life with its wealth, customs, laws, institutions, languages, religions, our autonomy? Or to protect the "material," i.e., economic conditions that support all these values? To affirm any form of life at all is at the same time to affirm the means to it; what *could* be more confused than to will our life and also to will the life opposed to it? The ultimate pacifist who would do nothing even to protect his own life for fear of killing another is simply a case of self-hatred; but both nature and logic combine to guarantee that this particular illness never becomes widespread. Has there been or could there ever be a defense for the idea that everyone else's life is preferable to my own, particularly when adopted in turn by everyone else? Being bound together in friendship is certainly preferable to being torn apart by hostility; but is it not clear that neither the friendship of all nor the hostility of all is possible; the line to be drawn that assures the provisional existence of any state is to be drawn by practical statesmanship judging in its time for its time, and not by abstract, would-be idealistic principles, which by hoping to be valid for all times are pertinent to none.

### EXCURSUS ON EQUALITY

No doubt it will have been noted that war here has *not* been justified as a means of securing justice or equality. It has been justified as a means necessary to any nation to secure or preserve its own social good and, as such, is held to be eminently reasonable and honorable. However, the social life of a nation is not itself to be further judged by means of abstract categories such as justice or equality. Hasty thought frequently identifies justice with equality, particularly since justice is elusive and protean in its applications, whereas the notion of equality, being mathematical and abstract, is within the grasp of all. I either do or do not have as much as another; if I do not, am I not wronged? Cannot anyone see this? And indeed they can, but what cannot be so immediately seen is whether such inequality is also ipso facto unjust.

These confusions pour into those discussions which, for example, would justify any war at all against the United States; since we have more than anyone else, we could never have a right to defend that more. To have more is to be guilty before the abstract bar of Equality. But this last gasp of the French Revolution, amplified by Marxist bellows, blows against certain existential realities. Those realities are simply that the earth itself is differentiated by rivers, climates, flora and fauna, mountains, valleys, and plains. Not all can live everywhere nor is this an injustice to them. And, to belabor the obvious, men are not equal, having very different temperaments, tastes, ideals, and histories. Not merely are men not equal, they are not inequal either, the category of "equality" being quantitative, whereas a man or a nation is not a quantity of anything but rather an individual or communal person aiming at a definite form of excellent life. Since nations and men are always already in a differentiated possession of the goods of the world, differentiated forms of excellence, differentiated histories and memories, the desire to equalize all is equivalent to the desire to obliterate history as well as the individuated free choices of nations and men. Computerized thought might delight in such simplicities, but is there any a priori reason why a truly just mind must accept it?

If I have not used the notion of justice in any abstract form to justify war, again, it is for the simple reason that it leads nowhere. Wars are fought *over* differing notions of justice; does any party to war ever think itself unjust? Justice in the abstract therefore is useless for purposes of condemnation or justification. Victory in war equally does not decide what is abstractly just, but which form of justice will prevail.

## Objections to War

### WHAT THE "PEOPLE" THINK OF WAR

I shall use this title for a slippery mass of appeals increasingly popular in the mass media. Reporters, seemingly getting the "objective" facts, can always ask some fleeing peasants:

"Do you want war?" Of course the bewildered peasant replies that he only wishes to live in peace, that war has destroyed his family, his rice fields, that it is caused by "government," that he could live equally well under any regime, that in fact he does not know the enemy, or does, having relatives among them, etc., all of which is pathetic as much for the sufferings of the peasant as for the mindlessness of the reporter who imagines himself to be presenting an ultimate argument based upon "humanity."

Television, since it cannot picture any thought about war, is confined to showing what can be shown: the dismembered, burned, legless, eyeless, as if to say: this is what war really is. And when the dead or wounded are little children, women, or old men, the very heart recoils; the argument is decisive. But not yet: the soldiers must be asked; have they not seen it firsthand, fought it with their lives, seen their comrades fall before their very eyes? Any number can be rounded up to swear they haven't the faintest idea what all the killing is about, that it must be immoral or absurd, probably conducted by munitions-makers or politicians seeking reelection, in a word, by all that "establishment" in which they never participated much even during peacetime. Their own virtue is to be resigned, or, if they "think," they wear peace symbols.

As for the ideal component in war, the honor and courage of the soldier, that too is immediately debunked. "There's nothing heroic about war," says the soldier who may just yesterday have risked his life to save a comrade. War is nothing but living in the mud and rain, with poor food, disease, fatigue, danger, and boredom; is that heroic? His reticence about "heroism" is admirable; but we need not believe what he says. Since heroism is doing one's duty or going beyond it under extreme conditions, it is difficult to see how the difficulties diminish the accomplishment; without those difficulties, genuine heroism would be nothing but parade-ground heroics. But let us look in more detail at these arguments of the people.

The People: who are they? They are either citizens of their country or not; if not, they have no political right to complaint. If so, then their government is indeed theirs, and they have every political duty to observe its decisions or try to alter them legally. In any event, the people are all the people, not merely the peasants, and they are in their collective capacity *already* represented by their government, whose decisions they must respect as made by their legal representatives. If the people are in no way represented by their government, then the question shifts itself away from war to that of forming a representative government. In any event, war and peace are decisions that obviously fall to the national government and not to miscellaneous groups, random interests, or ad hoc political rallies. Nor, least of all, to the private opinions of reporters interviewing a few people, usually those with the least opportunity to consider and weigh what is at stake. To suggest opinion polls or referenda on these questions every month or so simply offers us the idea of another form of government altogether, an unheard-of populism which in effect negates representative government altogether and substitutes for it the ever-shifting voice of the street. And since that in turn clearly reflects the overwhelming influence of propaganda, immediate "democracy" of this order shifts the decision from government to the directors and voices of "news" media. It is hardly surprising that this prospect delights the media, but it is surprising that so many otherwise sensible citizens wish to shift their allegiance from their own duly elected representatives to the directors of news media whom they have not elected and for the most part hardly know, all the while imagining that this offers them an opportunity themselves to direct the course of events.

The truth is, unwelcome as it may be, that the People—ordinary housewives, factory workers, farmers, etc.—as fine as they may be personally, are in no position whatsoever to consider the wisdom of that very politics upon which their own lives depend. It is, naturally, for this reason that very few nations at all, and none of any importance, are run on any such scheme. It is precisely the responsibility of representatives of the people to occupy themselves with such questions, inform themselves, and circumspectly weigh the possibilities. The limits of experience and political habits of thought which more or less make the ordinary private citizen private at the same time warn us against encouraging any immediate or undue influence of his opinions on matters of state. What the people think is simply the repetition of slogans derived either from campaigning politicians or from their favorite newspaper. For some researchers the popular mind is a pool of infinite wisdom and goodness; in truth it is nothing but an ephemeral reflection of popular songs, sandwich-board slogans, newspaper headlines, and clichés. For the popular mind, "thought" is what can be written on a placard or shouted at a rally; for the reflective, thought is precisely what eludes this form of expression. Who has the wind to shout a *qualified* thought?

Nothing could be more dangerous than the enthusiasms of the people. Mad joy at the beginning of hostilities; and rage when the bodies are brought in, the expenses reckoned up. But of course this is precisely what is to be expected from the people, suggestible, flighty, and unused to either foresight or circumspection. As for the shallow notion that the people want only peace, that all peoples love one another as brothers, and that war therefore is imposed upon them from above—could one find any stretch of history or any segment of the world where these notions are significantly illustrated? The natural brotherhood of man? The natural goodness of the people? Indeed! One could far better argue that there is nothing whatsoever "natural" in man; the natural is exactly what man *decides*.

When we substitute for the people the common soldier, all the same applies. Their experience is always tempting to novelists, looking for the "reality" of war. The reality in question, it should be remembered, is the one they are best equipped to express with vividness: the day-to-day life in the foxhole or in the pouring rain, the mudholes, the terror, sickness, ambiguities of fighting life. It is easy for novelists to enter into the mind of the G.I. who is presented as seeing only what lies before his eyes: a dead friend. *That* is the reality of war; meanwhile at headquarters the colonels are arrogant, incompetent, not really suffering, but instead well provided with booze and whores, no doubt profiteering from the PX, and in cahoots with the government, known to be corrupt. No doubt all this is true enough from time to time, and no doubt anyone at all can sympathize with the sentiments involved. And no doubt at all, the same structure can easily be found in any civil society that ever was in peacetime as well. The question, however, concerns the exact pertinence of such considerations to the justification or lack of it for any given war. Since wars are fought in the first place not to make common soldiers comfortable, nor to make generals live the same lives as privates, nor to remove corruption in the armies involved, the only pertinence of such observations when true would be to improve the army, not to stop the war. And that a platoon leader does not know the whole strategy from his experience, that a general cannot perform his legitimate functions in the same state of exhaustion as the G.I., nor carry his maps and codes into the foxholes, nor subject himself to the same risks as the ordinary soldier are all obvious but no doubt at times escape the full approval of the G.I., which is why the G.I. is not a general.

Related is the curious popular objection that war is immoral because the soldier does not know his enemy *personally*. A German soldier of WW I in *All Quiet on the Western Front* receives a shock when, after killing a Frenchman, he realizes he never knew him personally. However, he would have received a greater shock upon recovering his wits when he realized that if he *had* known him personally and acted out of personal rage, his act would be radically transformed in meaning. From being a soldier doing his *duty*, he would be transformed into a *murderer*. But no doubt this distinction is too fine for those who love to talk of war as "mass murder," oblivious to all distinctions between on the one hand the legitimate duties of the police and soldiers, and on the other punishable murder. This essential distinction is obliterated in that higher pacifistic fog where all "taking of human life" is immoral. There could hardly be anything more obscurantist than the desire to obliterate all distinctions of roles and offices of men into that warm, personal, brotherly unity of "the personal." Generals receive criticism for not taking a "personal" interest in each of their troops; I, for one, would demote any who did. If some such thing is the philosophy of the best-seller, it is easy to predict that of the worst-seller: the wise general and the stupid G.I. In all of this it would hardly take a Nietzsche to perceive the influence of that old, popular motive, the resentment of authority. In the present instance it feeds pacifism.

Popular thought loves to "psych" its political leaders. In this, has it not been aided and abetted by the rise of psychological novels where the plot sinks into insignificance and the psychological analysis of motives occupies the stage, usually a popular version of Freud. Psychologizing has, undoubtedly, a limited relevance to political decision; national policies are at the same time policies of leaders, whose characters and temperaments are significant factors in their actions and reactions. Both Roosevelt and Churchill considered the personalities of Hitler and Stalin in this fashion, and if their judgments left something to be desired, at least the pertinence of the question is undeniable; political personality is unquestionably a factor in objective policy. Which items in announced policy are sticking points, and which negotiable? Which remarks made to the inner constituency, and which to the outer world? Generals also try to sense the temperament of their opponents, as one factor in the whole.

On the other hand, what could be more ludicrous than the popular effort to assess policy through a judgment of the character and assumed private motives of the initiators of that policy? Antiwar finds nothing but reprehensible private motives at the root of the matter; prowar finds nothing but heroic strength; reflection finds both irrelevant. Wars are neither justifiable nor unjustifiable in terms of the private motives of the leaders; wars are not personal acts of rage and revenge, but, as von Clausewitz showed, an extension of policy by other means. Policies are measured by their probable costs and effects, and not by the motive of the agents.

The weighing of policy properly belongs in the hands of those responsible and thoughtful men who are experienced in such matters. It is not in any conspicuous sense the experience of pastors in their morality, poets with their sensitivity, the young with their idealism, psychoanalysts with their probings of emotions, or news reporters with their scoops.

The distressing thing about popular psychologizing is its confidence; it *knows* the black heart inside the political leader, and it is certain that anything more complex or even favorable is "naive." All of which reflects the failure of both psychology and the psychological novel to make their point; should not popular wisdom at least be sensitive to the difficulties and ambiguities of searching out the motives of the human heart? If I can only seldom if ever be confident I know my own motives, how can I be so sure I know those of others?

I conclude that the People must take their chances in war, that they do not represent a pool of persons separate from the organized body of citizens with a government, and that their perception, judgment, and analysis of public policy is sound only by accident. Public policy is beyond the scope of private people; since it is, the common people revert to something they imagine themselves to be expert in, the psychological motives of leaders; but, alas, even that is beyond their or anyone else's proper grasp. At which point we have nothing to do but return to what we should never have left, the objective consideration of policy by those competent to consider it.

### THE SUFFERINGS OF THE PEOPLE

A final set of criticisms against war again purports to rest upon humanitarian or idealistic grounds: its argument is the simple exhibition of death, injuries, disease, poverty, destruction, the ravaging of both countryside and cities. T.V. makes it as vivid as possible, and the color photographs in *Life* magazine are almost enough to sicken the heart of the bravest and to shake the firmest judgment. Indeed, this is their overt intention, and it is not long before they end up on pacifist posters as ultimate arguments. But of course arguments they are not, at best facts to be considered; but then who hasn't already considered them? Is there anyone who imagines war to be anything but killing? The decision to fight is the decision to kill; such a decision, needless to say, is never easy although it may frequently be justified. *If justified,* what service is performed by such direct appeals to vital instinct and sentiment? At best they would enfeeble our powers of judgment, never too strong, so that we would choose the unjustifiable rather than the wise course.

These images thought to be decisive are in reality nothing but kicks below the belt and from behind; reasonable moral judgment can never be a simple reaction to our emotions and sentiments; the emotions and sentiments themselves are more than enough for that; but it is the role of policy and judgment to judge *over* these forces. The job is no doubt the most difficult man faces; it is hardly made easier by the daily flood of images of suffering in the media.

The image in itself is no argument against anything. It would be easy indeed by vivid color photographs accompanied by recordings of screaming, wailing, and crying to sicken anyone of the very project of living. Surgical operations would never be undertaken, women would be afraid to give birth to children; images of the old, sick, and senile would convince us that life itself is folly; and some such thing is the conclusion of transcendental ascetics. But then such an ethic, by intention, is not pertinent to public policy, necessarily committed to not merely life, but the good life.

The humanitarian argument drawn from ruins and suffering aims at a higher idealism; but with a suddenness that would have delighted Hegel, it turns into its opposite, a crass materialism. If human life is justifiable in terms of its excellence, where is the idealism in locating that excellence in a clinging to cities and fields? Or finally, in clinging to mere life itself as our highest value? The founder of Western philosophy, Socrates, disdained to use arguments resting upon such sympathies in his own defense, and did *not* bring his wife and children to court to plead for him. Nor did he conjure up imaginative pictures of his own suffering. No doubt, this is old-fashioned. . . .

Since one dies anyway, the sole question would seem to be how one dies, with honor or not. There is no moral obligation to live at all costs and under any conditions; there is no moral obligation to live at all; there is a moral obligation to live honorably if one lives at all. What that obligation dictates under specific historical concrete circumstances clearly cannot be decided for all and in general; but it can dictate that under some circumstances some men must find their honor in defending unto death what they take to be more valuable than sheer existence, namely a human life dedicated to excellence and dignity. Human lives whose chief moral defense is that they have kept themselves alive have at the same stroke lost *all* moral defense. Such is the age-old paradox of life.

Traditionally, the man who chose life and personal safety under any conditions was regarded as a coward, and his condition that of a slave. Do we now have new reasons for reversing this decision? Which is not to say that some have not tried; what other judgment could be pronounced upon the current rash of movies and novels all celebrating the antihero as a new form of excellence; sometimes it is even thought to be "authentic" or "existential"! What is it but mediocrity and cowardice? It follows that some are authentic cowards, but need we admire them? A footnote to the present confusion is the argument that war "brutalizes" the troops. The brutalization is rarely spelled out although hovering around the attack is the suspicion that troops are brutalized in their coarse speech, their terms of contempt for the enemy, their failure personally to consider the "justice" of every order, their failure to bring their superiors before the bar of their own private conscience, their fondness for booze and camp-followers above lectures and the opera. Well! But if brutalization means a willingness to kill the enemy, I for one fail to perceive the fault; that's what they are there for in the first place, and who is closer to the brute, a man afraid to kill the enemy or one who will kill and die to preserve the freedom and dignity of himself or his compatriots?

There will always be occasions when human freedom and dignity are threatened; there will always be occasions, then, for a justifiable war, and the pacifistic argument fails. To attack the very idea of war is to attack something fundamental to the preservation of any honorable life and to offer under the flag of idealism or humanitarianism the very substance of cowardice. Having already denounced Soviet injustice, what could be a worse capitulation than Bertrand Russell's slogan: "Better red than dead"?

## What War Decides

Needless to say, victory does not always fall to the just. And if not, then victory is no measure of the justice of the cause, a truth commonly recognized by the respect accorded to the defeated. For while they were indeed defeated with regard to the immediate occasion of the dispute, they were not defeated, if they fought well, with regard to something far more important, that infinite self-respect which defines their humanity. The morale of a nation, that is, its self-respect, is certainly tested by the war, and it is that factor which nullifies the old Chinese warlord "solution" to the problem of war, much beloved of computer thinkers. Why not, the argument goes, have the leaders meet on a neutral ground, calculate their resources, and decide victory without bloodshed, as the story says the warlords did? Is this not the essence of "rationality"? If the idea seems preposterous, is it not because there remains one incalculable factor, the morale of the troops and the nations behind them? No doubt this factor was negligible when the troops in question were mercenaries without any morale whatsoever except that for their pay or "professional" reputation. And no doubt one can easily find battles when the odds are so unequal as to render armed resistance suicidal. But even such suicidal resistances *win something*, namely, the enacted courage unto death of the men fighting them; to think nothing of this or to regard it as pure folly is itself a judgment proceeding out of little but crass materialism. To offer it as a rational *idealism* is a betrayal of everything noble in the defeated. A man is not necessarily ignoble because he was defeated; but he is if there is nothing he will fight for except his own skin.

Courage then, about which little is said today without an accompanying smirk, is a virtue whose analysis quickly carries us into transcendental realms. It looks like madness or vanity or an "ego-trip" to those who imagine the issues of life settled, and settled into the values of biology, economics, or pleasure. But courage puts all those values into question, discloses that, as always, men today put to themselves a goal and destiny that has no common measure with mere life, mere well-being, or mere comfort. These things may properly be fought over, but they are not *in themselves* the full story of what is involved. That full story can never be told, but at very least it must include what here is called the transcendental, the domain of freedom and dignity that is never compromised by mere death, poverty, or defeat; but most certainly is compromised by a certain deafness to its claims. Wars are not fought to prove courage, but they do prove it all the same.

# Five

◇◇◇

# *The Death of Culture*
# *into Expertise*

### *In General*

THE CULTURE of the Western world has for some time been under diagnosis as though it were a patient sick with an unknown disease. The doctors are agreed only on this: the illness is acute. They differ on when it began, and how long the patient may be expected to live; they differ on how radical the cure must be. But, for a long time, no one has been very happy with it. Hegel, Marx, Kierkegaard, Nietzsche, Matthew Arnold, Spengler, Eliot, Jaspers, Marcel, to name a few, all find something radically wrong. Some, like Hegel, had the sense of living at the end of a great period, a twilight in which they could reflect on the work of the day. Others, like Marx, thought they could perceive the cause in socioeconomic factors which were correctable by revolution. Kierkegaard and Nietzsche saw the sickness in religious terms; Kierkegaard in the progressive loss of individuality, inwardness, and passion; Nietzsche in the "herd-men," the "nay-sayers," and he prophesied something beyond man, superman, who could at last affirm himself and life. But all the doctors feel that something is *finished.*

The subject is, of course, vast, and no one can hope to see more than can be seen through a tiny crack. Each must make his own diagnosis from his own peculiar standpoint, and that is what I shall try here. There can be no harm in looking once again at what passes for culture, estimating it, and pronouncing our own death sentence. My purpose, however, is not altogether negative; for although culture may be dead, the human spirit is not. If it is not altogether futile to dream, perhaps something better can be hoped for. At the end, then, I shall express my private dreams.

What, then, is culture ideally, and why is Western culture dead? It is clear at the start that we are not talking about culture as a leisure time activity, as entertainment alone; nor simply as that part of the communal work which never earns its own pay and must therefore be supported by tax-exempt donations. Nor is it an affair of snobs. Nor exclusively of universities. Nor of impresarios. There can be no question of isolating it on one page of the newspaper, or of escaping it altogether. For culture in its deepest sense is the whole life of the human spirit in communities. There is no sense, therefore, in seeing culture as only one part of that total life; or rather, when it appears in that light, something is radically wrong with the culture in that community.

Human culture, of course, is not something which has its own independent existence. It is not a rock formation that requires little or no attention, that simply *is*. It is a product of the human spirit, and that particular sort of product which is never finally produced; that is, culture is nothing but the *life* of human beings, and for culture to be alive means that actual human beings live it. Culture, then, is that medium which the human spirit creates for its own life; looked at objectively, it is found in the works of the spirit, in language, customs, institutions, as well as buildings, monuments, works of art, and symbols; but subjectively, all of these must be lived in. The accumulation of unread books may be important to a statistician, but those works have not entered into culture until they are read.

The human spirit, then, cannot take itself for granted. It may be found in all men and at all times but what is then found is nothing but potential spirit. For its *life*, it must act; and its action is its life within culture. And so while the planets need not give themselves the slightest trouble over their movement, the spirit must; it is alive only when it is creating its own life. That life is not automatic, nor instinctual; it must be created by the spirit itself. Hence, since the spirit is alive only when it is creating itself, the very life of the spirit is dependent upon its *concern*. Its concern is precisely for itself, for its life, for that life is only possible as a free effort. Concern is one fundamental feature of the spirit, but it should be noted in addition that the concern in question is conscious though not necessarily self-conscious. The spirit *is* nothing but consciousness, its life is conscious, and let it have what subconscious bases and memories it does have, it invariably must *seek* consciousness. It seeks to become lucid about what it itself is and what other things are. *Lucidity*, then, is a second mark of the spirit.

And finally, since the human spirit is inevitably in individuals, the life of the individual must *manifest* itself to others. In culture, each participates in the whole by encountering the expressions of others, and expressing or manifesting itself. Thus, the individual can emerge out of the limitations of his own privacy. In short, the life of the human spirit has three notable aspects: it lives only through its concern with itself, it lives or seeks to live on the plane of lucidity, and it expresses itself in objective works. Now these three features are nothing but functions; functioning together, they create culture. But when they take on a pseudo-life of their own, and desire to become distinct activities, professionalized and definable in themselves, we arrive at the contemporary scene: *concern* becomes the special province of "religion"; *lucidity* becomes the special province of "science" and "philosophy"; *expression* becomes the specialty of the "arts." And, in a nutshell, this is our own diagnosis. What now passes for "philosophy" is not and does not aspire to be a lucidity of the *spirit*. It is "technical," that is, pure knowledge devoid of any interest in the concerns of the spirit. What passes for religion is an "ultimate concern" that is not and cannot be made lucid by philosophy or science. And what passes for art is something thought to be pure expression, with no content, and above all no "message." The net result is that in aspiring toward absolute purity, toward independence, and toward the technical, these activities which might be the supreme expressions of the human spirit have achieved absolute triviality. They are, in our diagnosis, one and all *dead*. Worse, they are on the verge of becoming ridiculous. But before continuing with these bitter reflections, I should add that while I see little or nothing in the contemporary scene worth imitating or continuing, it would be both fatuous and ungrateful to ignore the genius that has gone into making it. Our criticisms are compatible with honor to the great; the creators of contemporary culture had very good reasons for what they did. But we must question whether those reasons are still valid, and whether we wish to continue in the same direction. And it should also be emphasized that there can be no question of imitating some past. If the present is not worth imitating, the past cannot be imitated. The truth is that no living spirit can imitate at all. We must not dream then of some "neo-," but rather of something genuinely new and genuinely old.

Meanwhile, there may still be a question in some reader's mind whether these noble activities are really dead. Perhaps the corpse still twitches. And so let us take a look at the contemporary philosopher, as he sees himself, and pronounce our judgment. And, sad as the picture is, as a professional philosopher I must include myself in the picture I am drawing; but my intent is neither confession nor accusation, but, I hope, diagnosis.

## The Technical Philosopher

Here I must beg leave to inform the general reader about technical philosophy, since he could not possibly know what it is unless he engaged in it. He most certainly will know the names of contemporary painters and composers; but will he know the name of a single technical philosopher? But this is more or less as it should be, as I shall presently demonstrate. Now, is the philosophy of the technical philosopher quite dead? Someone who could not read might gather that philosophy had never been more active. The number of articles published in our technical journals is staggering; no one could possibly read them all, or remember a single one. These articles, and not books, are our special product.

Professional philosophers are men and women who belong to professional associations, subscribe to professional journals, write these articles, reprints of which they pay for and send to friends, and who earn their living by teaching young people to do the same: write articles and teach young people to do the same. Altogether then we constitute a new phenomenon, the professionalization of wisdom. Let us take a closer look then at the Technical Philosopher.

First of all, his most characteristic temperamental trait is his extraordinary sensitivity to a certain criticism: that of being "edifying." In our inner professional circles, a more pointed sneer could hardly be found than that a work is edifying and suffused with uplift. Such a comment has almost the force of revoking a philosopher's Ph.D.; the accused winces inwardly and can only clear his name by writing not one but several articles for the *Journal of Symbolic Logic*. These articles, however, need not actually be read by his colleagues; everyone knows in advance that there could be nothing edifying in the pages of the *Journal of Symbolic Logic*.

The criticism of edification or uplift is particularly cutting since it touches upon the intent of the philosopher; no one can be edifying unless he intends to be; and it is this intent that represents a disloyalty to all the values of Technical Philosophy. There is another criticism, not quite so devastating since it does not concern itself with one's intent, but only with the worthlessness of one's accomplishment: and that is "muddleheadedness." In the view of Technical Philosophy, all traditional philosophy was muddleheaded, had no idea of what it was doing, and did even that badly. Muddleheadedness is almost a style of thinking, the old style, and is exactly what might be expected of a philosopher who intended to be edifying. For the most part, one need only read the titles of the classics in philosophy to perceive the muddleheadedness from which they sprang. Sometimes the very face of the philosopher is enough; a muddleheaded philosopher will have a softer face, there will be less aggressiveness in it, and sometimes a trace of serenity.

What, positively, does the new Technical Philosopher desire to be? Well, of course, technical, that is, scientific above all.

He wishes to regard himself as a philosophical worker, or even "researcher"; his work is thought of as a "research project," and if he can concoct a "cooperative research project," he will have no difficulty whatsoever in getting a grant from a foundation. Cannot many think better than one? Has not cooperation proved beneficial in the sciences? If the Technical Philosopher did not retain some faded memory of his tradition, he would be delighted to teach his classes in a white laboratory coat; instead he carries a briefcase.

His inquiries, investigations, and research will be embodied in a "monograph," a short paper with the "problem" clearly stated at the beginning, and at the end a summary of the "results." The monograph must also refer to the other "literature" on the subject. The Technical Philosopher thus is short-winded; he has an instinctive distaste for the sprawling works of the nineteenth century, when philosophers sometimes sought a larger view of things. One of the most influential of the new philosophers was Ludwig Wittgenstein, whose books were composed of separated pithy sentences and paragraphs, each of which is numbered for easy reference. This unfortunate man did not live to see his work undone; for now each sentence is being reinflated back into an article for the journal *Mind*. Close to the fear of being edifying is that of being a windbag. The Technical Philosopher feels that everything can be said quickly and to the point. At the meetings of his professional associations, papers are limited to twenty minutes. The president alone can speak at greater length, but since he speaks after dinner, he is obliged to devote a third of his time to telling jokes. And here I must add my own note of approval; when we have nothing to say, surely twenty minutes is not too short a time in which to say it.

The new style of Technical Philosophy is remarkable since it expresses something about the philosophy itself. The style tends toward the telegraphic code. One reason for this is that the paper must be capable of being read during office hours, and make no demands upon the weekends. Technical Philosophy, the reader must understand, is simply one sort of work for which one is paid. It should have no resonance beyond those hours. When carried to ideal perfection, it is expressed in some form of artificial symbolism, which takes years of training to read with any ease. The Technical Philosopher has always envied the mathematician, with his proofs and symbols. And he has always had a fear of natural or ordinary language. Ordinary language is so obscure; words come dripping out of a sea of feelings and related meanings, and are logically unmanageable. Therefore, we have devised a new language, symbolic logic, which begins with marks having no meaning at all; whatever meaning they acquire is given to them by other marks, which serve as their definitions. Now everything should be clear, and to some extent it is; but unfortunately the language is so impoverished that nothing of any importance can be said in it, and so artificial in form that error is perhaps more frequent in it than in our mother tongue.

One of the most desirable features of symbolic logic in the eyes of Technical Philosophers is its impersonality. It states the pure core of the argument with no emotional nonsense. The writer is invisible behind his symbols, although some who wish to be extraordinarily sensitive profess to be able still to detect personality now in terms of the "elegance" of the proof. But I do not know if this contention has ever been thoroughly tested. The Technical Philosopher detests "style," for he sees it as expressing personal attitudes, and what difference can they make? Style in an argument is as disturbing and inappropriate as perfume or sweat on the eyepiece of a telescope. The Technical Philosopher desires to *be* impersonal, to write impersonally, and to disappear entirely into his analyses. And to a surprising degree he succeeds, for, to be frank, there isn't much to disappear.

Now these various stylistic features of Technical Philosophy are not accidental peculiarities. They all flow, as I see it, from the substance of the philosophy itself. And so perhaps it is time to look at it. Professor Morton White characterizes our age as the age of "analysis"; and this is exact, unfortunately. The general reader may be tempted to confuse analysis with psychoanalysis; and that would be a mistake. What the philosopher "analyzes" today is not the psyche, but rather words, phrases, sentences, arguments, which purport to say something meaningful or true. The Technical Philosopher finds everything said more or less confused and unclear. And if you are not initially confused, there is no one like a good analyst to demonstrate the confusion that lurks in the most innocent phrase; and there is no question whatsoever the Technical Philosopher can exhibit confusions that would have confused no one.

Technical Philosophy, then, is analysis. But what is analysis? There is no problem here; to analyze anything is to break it down, to dissolve it into its components, to reduce it from its initial totality into its ingredient parts. Then the parts are reassembled back into the whole, and lo! now, for the first time, we "understand" what that whole was. But in all of this, two aspects hit the eye. The first is the assumption that language is not clear in its first usage. It must be *made clear* by the analysis. The second is the fervent assumption that the philosopher himself is entitled only to analyze; that is, his work consists of tearing apart intellectually phrases others have put together. He analyzes syntheses but he makes no synthesis himself. Let us examine more closely both of these assumptions.

The first assumption that language is not clear in its direct employment has the consequence that only the analytical philosopher knows the clear meaning of what others are saying. But, then, if their initial language was unclear in the first place, how could the analytical philosopher know whether his analysis was right or wrong? And so we find in *Mind*, a leading magazine for such discussions, articles written about articles written themselves about articles, all agitating the question whether an analysis really gives us the original meaning. Now if the original meaning was clear itself, what *need* for the analysis; and if it was not clear how could one *verify* the analysis? But the New Philosophers somehow succeed in *making* original utterances unclear in order to clear them up. This activity itself breaks down into two schools; one finds that all ordinary language is obscure, and can only be made clear by translating it into some artificial symbolism. These philosophers are called "ideal language men." A second school is antiphilosophical, and finds that all *philosophic* problems are generated by misunderstanding ordinary language. They "clarify" traditional philosophic problems by showing that there was no genuine problem, only a misuse or misunderstanding of ordinary language. These philosophers are called "ordinary language men." Now the result of both schools is that the new philosopher need know in his professional capacity *absolutely nothing* except how *words* are used. For all Technical Philosophers feel that there are but two matters of concern to knowledge. There are the "facts," and there is the question of how to express these facts clearly. The Technical Philosopher prohibits himself professionally from arguing "facts." All facts are to be drawn from the "sciences," which is another department of the university. And so he has nothing to do but analyze *language*, in a professional indifference to facts. Most of analysis, then, consists of analyzing the language other and more traditional philosophers have used. Here there are no facts.

Now the second aspect of the whole matter is that the Technical Philosopher makes no syntheses himself, i.e., he has nothing to say. This, of course, takes its toll on our mood. For as Technical Philosophers, we can never really say anything new by ourselves. Others have to say it first, and then we *analyze* what they have said. This means we can never speak first, and must wait for somebody else to provide a sentence or phrase which can then be analyzed. And too often it turns out that there is nothing to analyze. The first sentence was perfectly clear to all present except ourselves; and so our analyses have only the function of demonstrating the obvious or explaining the joke. Hence our bad temper. Further, our entire attitude toward sentences is *hostile;* we live in the mood of the hunter stalking the big kill, the phrase which is ambiguous or which contains, in the words of Gilbert Ryle, a "howler." This analytic hostility is, obviously, incompatible with love, with serenity, and with any comprehension of those meanings and subtleties which presuppose sympathy and love for their very sense. No wonder our brows are furrowed, our eyes narrow and glittering, our lips thin and compressed and already twisting into a smile of derision before the sentence is finished; we have detected a howler! The old style of serene sage has definitely disappeared from the scene. The ethic of the New Philosopher was expressed by Morris Cohen in his famous reply to the question why he was always critical: "It is enough to clean the Augean stables." But then the question remains as to the definition of dirt; precisely what is to be cleaned out? The New Philosopher wishes to clean out everything except what the scientists say or what he supposes "common sense" to be. But there is a vast agreement that traditional philosophy is the very ordure which logical, scientific, and clearheaded thinking must flush away as speedily as possible. The British Technical Philosophers especially trust something they call "common sense"; their American counterparts dote on "science." But in all cases, the content of philosophy is not supplied by philosophy; Technical Philosophy has no content of its own. It is rather a gigantic hose designed to flush the stables of traditional philosophy. Or perhaps a flamethrower, turned not only on filth and confusion, but also on stables, horses, and finally the flamethrower himself. The Technical Philosopher is the point of pure negativity, an eye that would like to see pure light but cannot because of visible things. It is this final phase which is the death of philosophy as well as a darkening of the lucidity possible to the spirit. Philosophy has at last achieved the pure heights of having no content, nothing to say, and nothing to do except analyze the confusions in what others say into an unintelligible jargon of its own.

To ask a Technical Philosopher for his vision of the world is to throw him into the worst of embarrassments. It is hopelessly to misunderstand what philosophy now is. The philosopher's answer will not try to supply that vision, or even recognize its absence; rather it will analyze the meaning of your question in order to show that it really has no meaning at all. It is left for others to supply the vision.

In summary then, the Technical Philosopher analogizes himself to the scientist. He wishes to be brief, technical in style and subject matter, impersonal, unemotional, and unedifying. He does not expect the layman to understand what he says, and would be slightly embarrassed if the layman did. He has nothing positive to offer, no vision of life or the world, no summary attitude or total view. His positive activity is to

analyze statements made by others, but never in his professional role to make such original statements himself. He
assumes that somehow or other the accumulation of these
technical analyses in the library adds up to something of value.
The New Philosopher does not wish to speak of matters of
human concern. He only wishes to be clear about little things.
He does not believe in his heart that one can be clear about big
things, or that philosophy should address itself to human
concern. One of the classical works most in disrepute today is
Boethius' *Consolation of Philosophy*. The Technical Philosopher knows analysis will bring no consolation. He is not the
pompous philosopher of the old style; rather, he regards
himself as a technician who "does philosophy" more or less in
his office during school hours. Weekends are another matter, a
vacation from philosophy.

Now this was not always so. For the longest stretch of its
history, philosophy was, embarrassing as it is to Technical
Philosophy, concerned precisely with large visions and the
edifying. That is, it was concerned with the human situation
and what was to be done about it. For traditional philosophy,
as well as for religion, man was regarded as a suffering animal,
not merely suffering in life from correctable ills, but suffering
from life, from the intrinsic and inevitable ills. Philosophy did
not specifically address itself to the particular evils in life, such
as sickness, poverty, war, and tyranny. The point of view of
philosophy was that even if all these were corrected, we
should still be suffering spirits. In short, man seeks some way of
saving the meaning of his life in spite of his death, in spite of
his guilt, pain, and misery. Philosophy then had its own proper
mode of salvation, which was not to live an imaginary life in
some beyond, nor systematically to blind oneself to the
necessary pain of living, but to comprehend the *meaning* of
these things. Philosophy has always been in a more or less
gnostic tradition, by which man could save something from the
wreck of his life by comprehending it. The mode of salvation
offered by philosophy was called *wisdom*, and philosophy is
named after its love. By wisdom alone can men rise above
dumb and meaningless suffering to a comprehension of its
meaning, and that comprehension was the comprehension of

something eternal and blessed. Now, all of this is edifying, of course, and moves within the circle of ethical, religious, and esthetic categories. The various "answers" to the question of the "meaning" of life given in philosophy center on the notion of truth; and philosophizing implies as its necessary precondition, as well as aim, an alteration in *attitude* toward life. And this is the pure edification worked by truth. The formulations of the end of meaning are various: "spectator of all time and existence," "the flight of the alone to the Alone," the "intellectual love of God," "*amor fati,*" "participation in the Absolute Idea," etc. They are not so various, however, but what they do not express a common meaning, the sense that human life culminates ideally in a lucidity about itself and its highest concerns. Wisdom was never merely a doctrine, although it had its doctrines. It was rather a pursuit of that height of soul from which the last truth could be seen. Now obviously such matters are not fit topics for Ph.D. dissertations, classroom examinations, or "technical analyses." For it is not open to anyone equipped with nothing but the criteria of logic to comprehend the sense of philosophy; in addition, the "analyst" must have a trace of the love of wisdom himself. And so it is not surprising that Technical Philosophers find in traditional philosophy with its flights and soarings, its edification and enthusiasm, nothing but a muddle of banality and mystification. The ambiguities of traditional philosophy are maddening to the new philosophical specialists; but perhaps it was precisely these against whom the ancient doctrine wished to protect itself. How indeed can the same ultimate things be said to young and old alike, to wise and foolish? Better to speak in enigmas which in their very strangeness might suggest a meaning different from that which meets the hasty eye.

Technical Philosophy steers clear of wisdom. Or worse, it is convinced that there isn't any, or if there is, it isn't the philosopher's business. And so the "muddled problems" of traditional philosophy are translated into clear ones, into problems that can be solved by technical means, by objective action rather than any inner transformation. The suffering of life is thus analyzed into a series of correctable ills. If it is disease you mean, then medicine will find the answer. If

poverty, then social and economic measures are indicated. If
ignorance, then more schooling. John Stuart Mill thought that
these summed up human misery, and the remarkable thing in
such an analysis is that not one requires for its solution an
inner philosophic transformation of attitude toward life. One
need only remain exactly as one is, see things exactly as they
are now, and work out the answer upon which everyone can
agree. The fact that no philosopher ever regarded his philosophy as a spurious medicine, economics, or schooling gave him
no pause. They must have been muddled about their own real
intent. And what is left over after all the medicine, wealth, and
education have had their chance to work? A few minor matters
such as death, guilt, and the meaninglessness which is always
ready to rise up in even the happiest. And suppose disease,
poverty, and ignorance could *eventually* be eliminated, as
everyone must hope, what is to be done now when they are
not?

Technical Philosophers are silent on these matters, or
vaguely embarrassed. They have nothing to say. They have no
vision, want none, and more or less identify philosophic vision
with hallucination. As for "changes of attitudes," if these have
any importance at all, there are experts for them too. The
psychoanalyst is in best repute, but the flabbier Technical
Philosophers feel that this is what the preacher might be for,
with his tired old platitudes. In any event pure knowledge has
nothing to do here; it seeks absolute purity, absolute independence, and absolute irrelevance to anything anyone might
conceivably be interested in. Thus has a noble discipline
committed suicide.

### And Art and Religion

Philosophy as wisdom has been dying a long time; but what
about art and religion? When we think of the images they once
gave of the mystery of human life: Oedipus, Antigone, Medea,
Hamlet, Lear, Faust, Ahab; or the gods, heroes, and horsemen
of the Parthenon; the faces of Rembrandt, the crucifixions of
Grünewald, El Greco. . . . And what were these but the
human spirit seeking and giving expression to its ultimate

clarity about its ultimate concerns? Here there was no question of "pure composition," of "pure expression," or even of the purely "esthetic." They are least of all "sensuous surfaces." The truth of the matter is that while these mysterious images are typically regarded as "art," they are just as much wisdom and religion. Now, the complaint is not that art today is "not as great" as it once was. It is true that it is not; but such judgments remain vacuous unless the question is transposed from the level of accusation to that of principle. There can be no question but that the human spirit potentially has the same eternal depths as always. If its results are incomparably more trivial, it is not due to lack of genius; but it may be due to certain directions taken individually and culturally, to certain *ideals* now dominant, which require examination in art as they do in philosophy. Is it accidental that the most creative painter in our day no longer seeks to give an image of the human reality, but contents himself with images of its distortion; and that when he is moved to express what he sees of life it comes out as the melodramatic slaughterhouse of Guernica? Or is it accidental that this passes for his "human concern," his "insight" into the human reality? But since when has wisdom resided in an intensity of outrage over physical destruction? If we should finally lose our minds over malice, cruelty, and destruction, would that be the ultimate achievement of insight and wisdom? The perception of evil some time ago was regarded as the bare *beginning of the problem*.

But then the contemporary arts are not noted for their images of the human reality. In place of such muddles, we find the ideal of "pure expression." The arts must free themselves from foreign emotions, associations, content, "reality," and become what? The purely optical, auditory, verbal? An entertainment for the senses? In literature it used to be Mallarmé, Gertrude Stein, and the puns of Joyce. But we needn't limit ourselves to the passé. The same phenomenon occurs whenever literature aspires toward pure style or whenever we see the emergence of the "professional writer." Professional artists of whatever sort are those whose profession is measured by skill in the manipulation of their respective media. The writer is measured by his ability to use words; but words, unfortunately, are symbols of something that is not words. That of which they are symbols is, of course, their content, but content for the professional is a matter of indifference. As a painter, he can equally well do a wine bottle, a scrap of newspaper, or the human face. And so indeed he can so long as the human face is seen as a composition of "lines and planes," since it has this and this alone in common with everything visible. And, so long as we are interested only in compositions of lines and planes, light and shadow, we may as well suppress the human face altogether; it is but a "literary association," or a "photographic" residue; pure creation will create with nothing but color and shape, and all it will create will be color and shape. The writer similarly will be able to write equally well about anything. His prose or poetry will be judged on its own merits; and what are these merits when we have abstracted from their reference to what lies out beyond them? Nothing is left but their "rhythm," "organization," "color," "originality of expression," "style," in short, everything but their truth and content. It is as if one were to judge a dinner exclusively by the plates on which it was served.

And since it is not possible to remove all reference to the human reality, there will be a trace of interest left in the content, that is, in what is exhibited of the human spirit. But since there is now no communal religion or philosophy that might extend the private sensibility of the writer, he must, if he is honest, fall back on his private imagination and feelings; and here we see again and again the impoverishment which the purely private brings. The honest feelings the artist finally discovers within himself, insofar as he rejects what light philosophy and religion might ideally offer, are not higher or more sincere or deeper truths; most frequently they reduce themselves to our old friend, sex.

Without extending the discussion endlessly, the same phenomena can be indicated in the other arts. Music in its turn also desires to be pure music, pure composition, to have nothing to do with "emotion," which is always "extra-musical." When emotion is mentioned, the opponents of it point to the most flagrant examples of Tchaikovsky; is that what is wanted? Or perhaps program music, where the title and accompanying notes *tell* the listener what to feel? And since no one could argue for any such thing, the conclusion is drawn that emotion as such is foreign to music, or music has its own pure emotions. Now the composer is thought of as a species of engineer either tailoring his composition to one record side, to an accompanying film, or, if these frankly external limits are abandoned and he is a pure composer, then the "composition itself" dictates its own form. But, of course, notes and scales do not and cannot dictate what is done with them, any more than words can dictate what is said with them. At best they set certain negative limits. The result is that "pure composition" is a radical absurdity, and as meaningless a phrase as "pure expression." The only practical result of such slogans and phrases is to divert the attention of the composer from the significance that emotion *musically expressed* might have, from the possible depths of emotion, to a pursuit of "pure" music, or compositions which are as devoid of feeling as possible; this leaves us on the one hand with paper compositions, supposed to be deep because nothing whatsoever can be felt through what is heard and where the chief delights derive from conceptual patterns emerging from a study of the score, or, on the other hand, the delights of purely *aural* contrasts, music which is little but orchestration, a composition of timbres, rhythms, and sudden dynamic shifts, an art of concocting thrills for the ear or tests for high-fidelity phonographs.

In our critical mood, we may as well look at what religion has become. Some men still take it seriously, bringing themselves to believe it still retains some trace of something or other of concern. But it can hardly be what is contemporary in contemporary religion that could command the slightest allegiance. For now we find the spectacle of a spiritual concern also trying to become a pure activity, and achieving little but absurdity. On the one hand, we find the universalistic tendency where each sect, confession, or denomination has lost confidence in its distinctive creed, and realizing that it is but one *mode* of religion, ashamed of its particularity, desires to become *religion as such*. "True" religion then from this standpoint is simply "having religion," a religion that is

indifferently Christianity, Judaism, Islam, Hinduism, as well as
Ethical Culture, Unitarianism, Christian Science and, so as to
be utterly free of prejudice, Atheism as well. Or, on the other
hand, sensing the absurdity of trying to speak a language that
isn't any particular language, religion reverts to its ancient
roots and becomes conservative, fundamentalistic, the religion
of "our fathers," a religion of absolute faith in a Founder,
Book, Church, or Tradition. Within this second tendency,
enmeshed as it is with dogmas, beliefs, customs, and words of
two or three thousand years ago, or the synthetic concoctions
of yesterday, incapable of winnowing the wheat from the chaff
for fear of dissolving into an indeterminate religiosity, a
peculiar doctrine emerges, that of "two truths." For now the
critical examination of "human" reason is feared; there is the
*sacred* truth, which must be believed in, assented to, to which
one must be "committed," versus a "secular" truth which is
but practical, merely scientific, and of course merely human
and relative. The former is holy, and touches everything
essential; the latter is useful, but subject to suspension by the
higher, sacred truth. One *believes* in sacred truth; one *proves
and demonstrates* secular truth. Everyone has seen the result of
this particular predicament. Fundamentalistic religions pass
imperceptibly and without the possibility of self-correction
into the blindest of superstitions, the chief pattern of which is
to see spiritual truths only as "miracles" in nature. Such a
religion, since it cannot employ the demonstrable insights of
reason except at its peril, has at its command no instrument
whatsoever by which to distinguish the authentically spiritual
from the childishly superstitious. Men are thought of as the
"children" of God or, worse, of other men denominated
"priests." If religion can use reason only to dissolve into a
general religiosity, when it dismisses reason it tends to freeze
into that impotence of the spirit called "commitment," or
"faith." The meaning of symbols is identified with the symbol
itself, and the more preposterous the result the more intensely
it must be "believed." Religion too in its contemporary forms
is as dead as philosophy and art; for just as nothing is so
characteristic of the contemporary philosophic mind as its
indifference to the spirit, nothing is so characteristic of the

contemporary religious mind as its indifference to both art and philosophy, and the resulting engorgement of an indigestible mass of unclarified and unclarifiable "beliefs." What else could result from an attitude where reason is regarded as "merely human" or relative, and inferior to the authentic voice of God himself who must lack reason, and art is regarded as pious decor, at best capable of depicting allegorically stories and commitments fixed in advance and without the contribution of art? When will religion regard the contempt of reason and of art as *blasphemous?*

In sum, then, contemporary Western culture in its most characteristic manifestations presents us with the spectacle of various functions of the spirit seeking to become autonomous activities, technical, professional, and separated from one another. The whole spirit is to be found in none of these activities, and eventually everyone at last becomes *bored* with them. There is, of course, a superficial activity in all three, and the statistics reveal an "increased interest" in them in the United States; but what figures could be more ambiguous in their meaning? For our part we find nothing significant or particularly valuable in frenetic efforts that express a distracted and bewildered spirit. In fact, it probably is the case that the more the spirit tries to divide itself, the more active it must become, the more frenzied, until it sinks at last into paralysis.

Now, to revert to our first considerations, the death of explicit culture has most important consequences. If the human spirit must live in the medium of culture it creates for itself, when that medium no longer can command honest allegiance, the spirit reverts into its own dark potential nothingness. If the spirit finds nothing of its genuine concern clarified and articulated in philosophy, what can it do but shun reason as such, look upon it as merely verbal, irrelevant, and logic chopping? When philosophy disappears as an effective clarification of ultimate human concerns, religion becomes anti-philosophical, and sinks into blind commitment; and art reverts to pure expression, which means either an expression of the sensuous or the inexpressive as such. In the absence of philosophy, the individual human spirit sinks back into a reliance upon the senses and the individual sciences for its light. When reason goes out, the senses and technical know-how are always ready to take over; they at least can operate without the effort at self-creation. When religion becomes preposterous, the honest spirit finds its concern in the instinctual and the appetites. They too need no effort to sustain them, and can provide a facsimile of life. When art no longer presents us with the image of the spirit, the spirit sinks back into the unexpressed; art becomes mere art, and expression or objectification is regarded as trivial. The inner life of the spirit is thought to be higher than its overt expressed life; and that inner life, distrusting expression as falsification, becomes mute and eventually shrinks to nothing. When culture becomes inauthentic the spirit reverts to the irrational, instinctual, dark and mute; this is as close to death as the spirit can come.

### Some Dreams

Providing there is any truth in all of this, the next question is what is to be done? But before exploring our dreams, we should be well aware of our limits. A living and authentic culture is not the product of individuals nor can it be planned in advance, particularly on the basis of a dead culture; nor when it emerges will it take any form necessarily recognizable to us today. There can be no question therefore of dictating where the free and concerned human spirit shall go. Nor of offering concrete suggestions, or attempting to create a new culture tomorrow. But perhaps it is not wholly foolish if we let our dreams wander a bit to explore at least some *directions* counter to those embodied in our present culture. For while the communal spirit does not operate and should not operate by technical planning, neither is it an instinctual growth like that of coral colonies. It is in the last analysis *consciousness*. And consciousness has the distinctive property of wishing to envisage its end, of taking thought of its goal while it acts. It is precisely the intent of contemporary culture that we find empty; it does admirably what it sets out to do, but is its aim anything of value?

The first remark then is negative. There is nothing viable in the present tendency toward the professionalization and isolation of spiritual functions. They dry up and become meaningless motions. Science in some of its problems can and must be specialized. But philosophy, religion, and art are not activities directed to specific finite aims but rather expressions of what is or should be a whole spirit. They are nothing but various functions of what is itself one. But this negative remark is insufficient.

Is the solution then to be found in an increasingly popular suggestion among educators, that these disciplines must be added to one another? But how can disciplines which are *set up* as separate be fructified by addition? Joint courses or combined curricula are mere shams if what are joined are themselves unjoinable. And, in addition, what profit is contemporary art to derive from contemporary philosophy or religion? None as I see it. And so with the other combinations of these disciplines. The matter lies deeper than this, and life is not generated by the addition of dead ingredients.

Nor is anything to be sought in revivals of the past. To revive the past is impossible and undesirable; even if it could be "revived," it carries within itself its own dialectic; we should be reverting to a simpler and happier age only to run through the course of history a second time, with minor variants. In short, there was an inner reason for our present predicament; the disease is not to be cured by reverting to its earlier phase. But more importantly, no living spirit can *imitate* anything; its life is precisely its creativity. Hence, everything properly called "neo-," "neo-conservatism," "neo-liberalism," "neo-thomism," "neo-realism," "neo-symbolism," "neo-primitivism," or "neo-whateverism" must be excluded from our attention.

But similarly, merely to notice the schizophrenia in the modern spirit is negative and insufficient. Nor will the "interrelation" of functions themselves be any new direction. To relate three functions of the spirit to one another may be a

necessary condition for health, but the substance is still lacking
from our analysis just as it is from contemporary culture itself.
If the functions can be defined as *concern, clarity,* and
*expression,* joining them together still omits any mention of
their proper reality: *what* is it that is to be clarified, with
which the human spirit is concerned, and which must be
expressed? What is the substance of the human spirit? Can
the question of culture receive any answer whatsoever that
ignores this most difficult of all questions? And while it is
true obviously that the spirit *can* take an interest in *anything
whatsoever,* still those casual and miscellaneous interests cannot define its ultimate intent.

Now, it is precisely this living substance that must be
*created.* But, certain *general* things might be said in advance.
For what could the substance be but the life of the spirit itself?
In short, the human spirit is and must be concerned with itself
and its life. Now this formula may seem too anthropocentric
until it is realized that when the spirit is concerned with its
own life it is also concerned with the *absolute context* of that
life. There is no such thing as "merely human" life; life is
precisely human to the extent that it seeks to relate itself to
that which is not merely human but to what it can honestly
regard as *ultimate.* And so the human spirit is concerned with
its relation to what it sees as ultimate. And what if it sees
nothing as ultimate? Then also *that* is its ultimate vision, and
constitutes the absolute sense it makes of its life. Thus, with
Hegel, it can be said that the human spirit is precisely that
effort to clarify and express its ultimate concern, which concern is precisely the sense it can make of itself. And therefore human culture is an attempt to make *sense* out of its
concrete historical life, a sense that is lucid, ultimate, and
expressed. Now the sense need not be and never is in any great
culture a flattering of our desires or a consolation for whining,
meanings which are sought only in the decay of culture. But
ultimate sense it must be, if philosophy, religion, and art, and
with them individual human lives, are not to relapse into the
senseless.

My dream, then, is for a culture that again seeks to make
ultimate sense out of the human spirit and its concern with an

ultimate context. This would imply a philosophy that gave less attention to symbolic reformulations and would-be "technical problems" such as the problem of induction, the external world, other minds, sense data, and so on, but sought to clarify the concerns of the spirit. It would imply a religious sense that did not despise reason or did not harden itself within a commitment but could see the spirit in what it now regards as the "secular." And finally an art that expressed not expression itself but the image of the human spirit. Each of these functions can make indispensable contributions; but only when each works with its eyes on the others and also on their common substantial aim.

And it is here we must stop; for it is precisely the *content* of this new substance that cannot be anticipated. It is exactly this future sense of reality that must be created, and created from deeper dimensions of the spirit than the current professionalized activities now envisage. In a word, the task as it appears now is for culture to create a new sense of reality within which we can live without either pretense or suffocation.

# Six

◇◇◇

# *Beyond Civilization*

> In the beginning was boredom
> —KIERKEGAARD, *Either/Or*

### *Preliminary Note*

THIS CHAPTER is a response to an inquiry that asks the following questions:

> Is there an ideal kind of civilization? Can civilizations present and past be cross-culturally compared in terms of achievements and failures? Would the results of such comparisons be acceptable to most men? What would be the criteria or parameters used to justify such results? Can modern civilization be more or less preserved as is? Does it require reformation? Must it be scrapped and replaced? If something must be done, who are the ones who have the will, courage, and knowledge to maintain the present or produce a new civilization: are they humanists, artists, scientists, philosophers, the common man, a given social class or combination of social classes? Will there be a civilization of the future?

First, a brief response to these questions before turning to the *fundamental* question, the presuppositions of the questions themselves, in order to suggest a related yet categorically different *mode* of questioning. To the questions as posed, it would seem to me evident that since civilizations are themselves ideals, and since any civilization is a form of life, there could be no single "ideal civilization" any more than there could be a single "ideal person." And since civilization is a form of life, it is only accidentally measured by criteria such as achievement or failure, criteria meaningful only for activities that have a finite, assignable end. If life has no such assignable end, neither has civilization. Each life and each civilization proposes to itself its own ideal; beyond that, what have we but abstractions thought out by someone else, a "critic" of persons and civilization? Precisely from what platform would such a critic speak? Next, the aspiration to define an ideal "acceptable to all men" destines the project to disaster; have all men ever agreed on anything? Should they? Would the agreement of most be compelling on the rest? Have we not with this question covertly introduced criteria appropriate to a political rally into the domain of philosophy to the latter's sorrow? So far as preserving or reforming modern civilization, fortunately critics of that civilization have very little influence on their subject matter. Civilization everywhere and anywhere changes itself, preserves what it still has some heart for, changes toward what it still has hope in. And all of this occurs independently of the cheers or wringing of hands of private critics. Nothing alive stands still, nor does it turn itself inside-out into something unrecognizably different. With what would one "scrap and replace" one's own civilization except with what is already afoot in that civilization? Of course, "something must always be done," but that could hardly be either the invention of a new and unheard-of form of collective life out of whole cloth, or the imposition of a glacial immobility upon what is. Nor, of course, is the life of any civilization sustained or modified by the "will, courage, and knowledge" of anyone. If any civilization rested upon any such virtues, it already looks moribund; and if something new is to proceed out of will, courage, or knowledge, it had better look at once elsewhere for its motive power. Those virtues are indeed appropriate to individual acts, particularly those where knowledge has some role; but neither civilization nor culture is an individual act, nor are the ideals that define civilizations objects of anything that could even remotely be called knowledge. They are evidently ideals, and an ideal is an object of choice and devotion, not knowledge. And finally, "will there be a civilization of the future?" Who knows? The term "future" conceals a disquieting ambiguity: is it the *factual* future, to stare into which is both amusing and fatuous, or is it the *ideal* future, which is but another name for our hopes? Or is it a *dialectical* future, to which I shall turn in a moment?

In a word, the presupposition of these questions is insupportable. The civilization in which we live is not an entity independent of us from which we can, as observers, detach ourselves in order to judge it, preserve it, scrap it, or project out of private dreams something new to be brought into being by will, courage, and knowledge of the good. For a single person to examine his civilization, in order to approve this and reject that, is for him to offer us nothing but a moral profile of himself that may be interesting in its own terms, but not for the question he imagines himself to be addressing.

And thus, by mental formation, we are already in civilization perhaps as a resentful fish in the water, and if we were not, we would not understand the least thing about it. Our life does not offer its meaning to an a priori being from Mars; and civilization, whatever else it is, is a form of life. As a form of our very lives, it is nothing that can be grasped as a whole. It is not surveyable, conceptualizable, nor does it offer itself up either to experiment or to a priori insight, Husserl in his *Crisis* to the contrary notwithstanding. It is not, therefore, a directable process. Whatever understanding we have of it is by way of sympathetic participation, and that offers us only partial glimpses into something *essentially* unfathomable. These glimpses need not be delusive so long as we remember the surrounding darkness; but need we listen further to anyone who supposes himself to have *grasped* either life or civilization? Has he grasped either himself or a friend? Woe unto him if he thinks so.

It is not surprising, then, that the questions are all "civilized" questions addressed to civilized men, and that therefore they can hardly touch anything fundamental. Civilization, as we shall see, is in effect nothing but the very questioning of itself. But so long as it remains within the circuit of such questioning, it can only stumble about in the domain of personal preferences, empty hopes, contrary denunciations, self-hatred, or self-congratulation.

But fortunately none of us is wholly civilized. There remain, therefore, resources from which we might glean some suspicions of those origins and that future destiny of the civilization within which we are. These ideas of origins and destinies do not offer themselves as personal preferences, nor are they efforts to peer into a future of which no one knows anything. They place themselves on the plane of phenomenological and dialectical analysis; our questions now are: Why and out of what did the human spirit civilize itself in the first place? What is that into which it has civilized itself? And what can be envisaged as the *dialectical* future of the civilized spirit? The three aspects are all dialectical: that is, they name stages in the development of the human spirit. And since we all are in midflight, that is, civilized people, can we not by sounding out the depths of our own actual spirits find the secret motives through which *we civilized ourselves* in the first place, what it finally is to be civilized, and where we civilized men must long to go? Where that is will carry us almost wholly *out* of civilization conceived of as anything spiritually final. But this very project of archaeology, of uncovering deeper strata of the mind and its life, presupposes that these layers are all still present, waiting to be uncovered. The life of mind is itself dialectical, a developmental form of existence in which the past is not simply obliterated and unrecoverable except by inference, but rather still there, buried but active; and its future haunts it, not in any factual form, nor merely as a moral choice, but as already logically prefigured in the present, and therefore available to the conscious life that lives now. These presuppositions, which might seem highly questionable put so baldly, are in fact merely abstract descriptions of the very everyday and humdrum life available to any of us. The mind moves ahead, builds upon itself, and it retains implicitly its former explicit enthusiasms, and it already conceals within it something *beyond* its own explicit present. Needless to say, this way of uncovering the embedded logic of culture, civilization, and what lies beyond civilization owes its essence to Hegel; I should argue that some such thing is *all* that philosophy can say in response to the initial questions, even if it departs from Hegel's own analysis here and there. And, as with any phenomenological analysis, *facts* from here on are to be taken as illustrative rather than evidential.

### Nature and Culture

Nature is first, culture second, and civilization third; these are surely not related simply by factual succession or chance. Each presupposes what is prior to it for its basis and sense. And in the present case, the most difficult of all for us is nature. For if we try to elicit the sense of natural life in ourselves, we are at the very limit of our possibilities of excavation; is there anything whatsoever left in man of the purely natural? If we look in the direction of the "animal," self-protection, food gathering, and reproduction in ourselves, we find that these are already so modified by culture that the purely animal or "natural" is for the most part poetic, what other animals are to man, who is no longer an animal. We feel traces of ourselves in our pets and in the higher apes. Our pets take on something of our life and the higher apes almost begin to behave as we do. Some men even wish to become animals, but that nostalgia is itself strictly human. In any event, the life of animals is not conspicuously a life within a culture, and ours is. Human self-defense is not exclusively snarling and rage; feeding becomes dining; and lust is modified by love. Caves and nests become homes, a naked beast clothes itself, paws develop into hands that can make tools, snouts develop into faces, the body is tattooed and ornamented, hair is cut, the animal walks upright with some discomfiture and fatigue, ways of right behavior are established, ideals are proposed, grunts and signals become speech, a society is formed beyond the animal troop, gods are revealed and worshiped. The final step occurs when man *distinguishes himself* generically from the animal, even when he traces himself totemically back to some favorite beast.

The natural is for us a limiting idea; our own nature is no longer accessible phenomenologically, and the content of the idea is more or less drawn from our observations of and friendships with other animals. It is a fundamentally negative idea arrived at by an attempt to strip from our own sense of life all that can be accredited to culture, that is, all mental interpretation. I should say, therefore, that no man knows what it is like to be an animal or natural.

But we are in a far more fortunate position with regard to our own selves as participants in culture. Here we have but to elucidate our own lives as we live them, but with a far slighter qualification: that we do not attribute to *culture* that which properly belongs to *civilization.* For our purposes here, culture names a collective mode of life that is the work of instinctive mind; civilization is the work of mind no longer instinctive but consciously reflexive upon culture.

Culture, then, can be regarded as the work of mind, but mind working instinctively. It is not "natural" if that term designates life which while conscious does not yet exhibit in any conspicuous sense volition and deliberate thought. The natural world has desire and sensation, of course; animals are not asleep; but will and thought, not yet. While springing up naturally, those powers by their operations bring man out of the purely natural into the human, and with that man forms his own culture though hardly by any act of deliberate choice. The mind here works by its own instinct, and what is the instinct of mind but to plan and think, to raise to order that which before was simply given or found, merely natural.

The culture I have in mind is itself hardly to be found now except in primitive or degenerate forms in New Guinea, Australia, the Philippine Islands, etc., but are these not already essentially transformed by the attentions of civilized anthropologists? And yet some such thing is the basis of everything within history that developed into civilization. Can it too be excavated by dialectic, in order to respond to the question *why* did we civilize ourselves? And after that, what? But with culture we have something more accessible to us than the natural; even within civilization much of culture remains even though modified.

If culture is that form of collective life which proceeds out of the instinctive operation of mind, and if the primary acts of mind are will and thought, taken together, the aspiration of mind itself must be to raise the natural to the level of significance, to either impose upon or discover order within its own life. But mind, I think it safe to say, primarily never regards its own works as "imposed" by it; for itself, in its direct and instinctive force, it assumes it is *discovering* an order *already there*. It is only through a secondary reflection that it interprets its discovery as its own work. But that already belongs to civilization, to the reflexive examination of its own "work." But in the beginning, that is, in culture properly so called, mind works directly, or, as later reflection has it, "naively" or "instinctively." Needless to say, it does not regard itself as naive.

What is the "order" it discovers? That there is good and evil, that there are general connections among the events in its life, in other words, that what had been simply there is now felt and seen as *connected;* and connected in a form that is intelligible. Since it is intelligible, and since the mind of culture does not imagine itself as the source of order, that source is something like its mind but independent, divine, imperious: the old gods of nature and human life. The gods are origins, the very same who were the gods of one's ancestors, not in the least modern or private, gods who are the source by their own will of what is proper and what is not, of the fertility of man, beast, and crops, who are sufficiently different from ourselves to suddenly appear without any reason knowable to ourselves in the form of bolts of lightning, floods, droughts, who are sufficiently close to ourselves to be moveable by prayers and sacrifices, so long as they are performed in the old way and with a pure heart.

For culture this is the way things are; and it is best for man to live within an order which proceeds from the gods and which was discovered by ancestors, that is, from of old. To be human is to worship the gods in the old way. Culture, then, is that instinctive sense of coherence, significations, and order where mind is straightforward. Its will wills the objective, divine good; its thought thinks the truth, and its arts are at one and the same time useful and in the praise of the gods.

Life lived within the primary acts and instincts of mind is so foreign to us civilized ones, it might be well to pause here for a moment. It surely has been lost irrevocably. And if it looks hopelessly *primitive*, before we proceed to the delights of civilization there is room to ask precisely what has been lost. And I should argue that culture, defined as here, is the absolute basis of the true, the good, and the beautiful. Without culture the famous trio of values would lose instantly every shred of significance. They are all to be *essentially modified* in civilization; but then *what* is it that is being modified? To anticipate, the modification worked by civilization will be to place all these values within quotation marks.

But for culture, they are never within those brackets which evacuate them of their primary meaning. To understand the gods as "gods" is already blasphemy. Similarly, to speak of truth as "truth" is to turn it into falsehood. To speak of *both* truth and falsehood within quotes is to speak unintelligibly, although such is the inveterate practice of civilized philosophy. Some effort therefore is required to recapture the straightforward sense of life lived before civilization and upon which civilization lives parasitically.

Culture loves what it loves and hates what it hates and is certainly capable of perceiving inevitable conflicts between the two as well as dreaming of possible resolutions. It is by its own instinct *moral* where that term had not yet lost its concrete sense, or had not yet attempted to become formal. The famous question "why be moral" would be unaskable and senseless. The moral *is* what is right, not what I think right, and its rightness is directly connected with the gods. Religion and morals could not be separated; and the gods were the gods of always, of the ancestors, and they were least of all abstract principles, laws, or even scrutable by reason, the very exercise of which in this domain is impiety, arrogance, and human folly. Furthermore, the moral in culture is invariably *concrete*, ancestral patterns of how to live and what should be done. Hammurapi's Code and the Ten Commandments offer us almost pure examples. In the case of Hammurapi's Code the moral laws specify even the price of a bushel of corn and the precise penalties for cheating, as if they were to be fixed for all time. Freedom meant largely the release from slavery, and not the very essence of consciousness as it has come to be for

Sartre. Moral life then was inherently connected with custom, but custom was not understood as the sad chronicle of what men had done but as the best in what they aspired to do, and unexaminable by private persons. Neither Plato nor Aristotle wished young men to study the state with an eye toward its critique; they might have a pure reason sufficient for mathematics, but they did not have the concrete experience of life necessary to understand all those "reasons" for custom that cannot be reduced to or seen by abstract reason. Further, they lacked piety or reverence for the sources of life; they might even go so far as to dream that they had invented themselves. For final efforts to make sense of an inscrutable life, culture turns to its dramatists. *Drama,* because the subject matter is not private sensibility, but rather the social life of the group; that too must be seen, and seen from the point of view of the gods, who are both angry and amused. The dramatist, then, whether he writes comedies or tragedies, or neither but is rather a choreographer of customary rituals, is for culture the same as the priest or the philosopher. And the drama, the ritual, the dance, are never conceptual although they are indeed reflective. But the reflection now is not into abstractions, but into what the dramatist presents as a final concrete whole: what we men can see after all our wars, loves, and destinies are over. Some such thing is the instinctive life of mind that finds only a degraded echo in the life of civilization: now culture and its direct senses, problems, and celebrations are left only in the form of stale religious and national holidays, empty forms, hollow rhetoric, boring entertainment, all of which nevertheless can catch us by the throat for brief moments.

*Truth* for culture also means something radically different from what it means for civilization or abstract reflection. For culture or the instinct of mind, *to be true* is primarily the character of a *man* and not of *propositions*. In Anglo-Saxon, "truth" comes from "troth," which means loyalty and not propositional correctness—preserved in an obsolete form as "plighting one's troth." To be loyal, to be true, is obviously a *moral* value and not the product of intellectual cleverness. *Any* man is called upon to be true, by his lovers, friends, and community; it doesn't require a supreme act of "intellect." Its opposite is not the incorrect, but the disloyal, the lying, the cheating. Obviously here we are dealing with a very different category from anything widely studied in epistemology.

The instinctive acts of mind aim directly at their proper end; culture is our name for a social life and understanding based on that direct and instinctive aim. Culture then is the home of the true, good, and beautiful, as well as their straightforward opposites. Culture is that lost paradise which has always haunted civilization. Or it is that Golden Age which was "once upon a time," or will be in some unforeseeable future when civilization cures itself of its ills? And always there is the suspicion that civilization is itself the illness. Culture is not easily accessible to us civilized ones; we are too civilized within to find the straightforward instincts of mind lying ready to hand. Almost our entire impulse is to reflect them into something else, into reflexive instincts, which is precisely what they are not. Nor will history be of much help, since history itself is the product of civilization and therefore of least use precisely on those periods where written language was never or only occasionally employed, the period of culture. Surely we are closer to our primitive selves than we are with our natural selves, but still at such a distance that this stage is best illuminated not by analytic thought but rather by the dreams of poets.

Constituent of that dream of the Golden Age is the structure of the dream itself, taken as wish-fulfillment and not nightmare. The Golden Age was beautifully uncomplicated and self-sufficient; its people were noble, loyal, and devout, or if they were not, their crimes had a certain inevitability and magnificence to them. Meanness, small-minded cleverness, and endless deception are rare though there is a whiff of them too in Loki and even Ulysses; and there was a good deal of trickery on Mount Olympus, but then the Greeks loved agility of mind more than most. The arts of the Golden Age are beautiful in a simple and obvious way: finespun gold encrusted with the brightest and rarest gems, silver and marble, all turned to the purpose of temples, cups, swords, bracelets, helmets, harnesses. In the Golden Age men had a detailed knowledge of their natural environment acquired by experience and lore, hardly by experiment and analysis. Its social arrangements were fixed and satisfactory in form. There was always a question of who was to be king, but not of kingship itself. There might similarly be a question of whether justice was exercised, but not of what it was. Even the wars of the Golden Age seem in the poem to be rather more like gorgeous rituals than nasty bloody affairs among strangers. Victory was glorious, celebrated, and preserved in legend. All in all, the dream that for all we know may also have been true presents us with the *least-alienated man*. The history of the idea of the Golden Age has been well studied; Plato even has Socrates dreaming of it in the *Republic*; the good life before the soul became fevered with the desire for more than was either healthy or just. Christians and Marxists also spend a certain amount of their time in such dreams. The questions at the beginning of this essay are equally dominated by such dreams.\*

But our present problem is somewhat different from either a historical or a poetic one. Since culture, civilization, and the dialectical future of civilization are all considered here as layers within present consciousness, and therefore subject to excavation and articulation, our present question concerns the motivation by which the human spirit chose to depart from culture and civilize itself; and finally what lies beyond. The question is phenomenological; that is, the act of civilization is regarded as an act indeed, something with a sense, and not an accidental fatality that fell upon us as a result of chance discoveries in the natural sciences, the technology of metals, the discovery of suitable climates, trade routes, population expansions, or anything whatsoever resembling a natural process. It goes without saying that all these things occurred, and all had their influences upon life, such that now virtually the entire planet is civilized in some form or other. But to become enchanted by these phenomena as though they were causes is to forget certain essential facts about the human spirit as well as the essential phenomenon being questioned. Civilization is an *act*, an act of a very distinctive sort and an act of the human spirit. The acts of the spirit have an *intention* whether self-consciously known to it or not; the intention of an act is essentially and not accidentally connected to it, being, in fact, its very structure. And since the spirit is in varying levels and degrees conscious, its intentions are in principle accessible to its own reflective analysis. The question, why did the spirit civilize itself, is therefore in principle answerable and answerable by a reflexive return of the civilized spirit upon itself to discover that hidden intent. Needless to say, the project must always remain tentative in its results and sensitive to the very profound complexity of the problem. No one can grasp the problem in its depths.

The history of the histories of civilization would show them to be of little use for our project. What for us is a *problem* for them is presupposed in the form of some morality taken for granted. They are in effect concealed theologies. One class sees the origin of civilization in a Fall. The temptation to the knowledge of good and evil was accepted and with that men have been confused in mind, speech, and action ever since. Thus disobedience, greed, egotism, vanity, lust for power, sex, or curiosity, whichever the favorite vice of the historian is, "accounted for" the rise of civilization, "whose proudest virtues are but glittering sins" for Augustine. Or the morality shifts feet: men civilized themselves because of the obvious advantages: now the Garden of Eden is the scene of savagery, butchery, cannibalism, all of which are obliterated by civilization. Superstition gives way to reason and science, tyranny to democracy and law, the sway of tradition to a readiness to reform, disease, poverty, and hunger to public health, wealth, and an abundance of food. The wretched naked savages now have the opportunity to clothe themselves, feed themselves, and live longer than thirty or forty years. But here we are not interested in the "moral" evaluation of civilization. If it is a Fall, why indeed did men choose to fall? But if it is Progress, it is progress only into civilization and its own values, which can hardly help us with the question of why those unique values should be chosen. More importantly, the values of civilization are necessarily at the *expense* of other values realized better in simple culture, which accounts for the civilized nostalgia for the Golden Age. Morally considered, civilization is a highly ambiguous phenomenon; and it would take a hardy soul indeed to sum it all up as an undoubted triumph or failure. Finally, since so many of the triumphs of civilization are apparent only late in its development, how could they supply the motivation for its choice at the earliest stage? And so there is, at very least, room for further questioning.

### The Origin of Civilization in Boredom

The question may now be rephrased: what was lacking in the Garden of Eden? and the answer that seems to me most direct is *excitement*. Its happiness and virtue were insufferably boring. Men civilized themselves to escape *suffocation* by the Good, True, and Beautiful. But something should perhaps be said to save this answer from the charge of frivolity.

Civilization cannot be regarded simply as a prolongation of simple culture along lines already definable within culture. It is something else altogether, a radically different posture of mind that we shall call here "reflection." If the mind of culture feels, thinks, wills, and acts straightforwardly, the civilized mind never does, at least not in its capacity of being civilized. This is not to say that it is devious but rather that it is reflexive upon its own direct activities. It therefore does not worship, but sees itself worshiping; it neither loves nor hates, but critically notices itself "indulging" in these activities. Its own reason formerly directly addressed to problems now becomes suspect as the very source of the problems it formerly found in nature. Reflection is the doubling back of consciousness in any form upon itself; and with this doubling back, the individual self comes to self-consciousness. The "I" enters the stage as the central actor. For the instinctive acts of mind, there is a nature out there to be patiently and reverently explored, gods whose pleasures and angers are to be studied, other men who are to be loved and hated. The act of reflection radically transforms the scene; noticing that all of what had previously been regarded as "objective" is so only for some subject, and that it itself is that subject, the formerly objective world becomes now *phenomenal:* it is the mere correlate of my own or some other subjectivity. Things, nature, men, and the gods are for me what I take them to be; otherwise they lose sense, and indeed how can we think the unthinkable, experience the unexperienceable, or love the indifferent? This phenomenological reflex, which has been studied again and again, usually from idealistic or transcendental points of view, is at the same time not in the least a product of arguments, but a possibility always latent in the instinctive mind of culture and, when chosen, "when the temptation is accepted," we have by an inner act already radically transformed ourselves, our world, and our lives.

This act of radical reflection upon ourselves has been justified in a number of ways but always in my opinion inadequately. We are now, needless to say, already on the plane of what in late civilization is called "idealism" or now "transcendental phenomenology." The justifications of radical reflection follow a predictable pattern: it is only in reflection that we can finally achieve the truth of what we formerly took for granted. And the truth so seen is the destiny of European man, as Husserl defends it in his *Crisis.* For Hegel it is a necessary stage in the ultimate teleology of the spirit itself, whose goal is Absolute Knowledge. But in each case the new "truth" or the Absolute Knowledge attained is radically different from the old truth, which had nothing to do whatsoever with reflexive clarity. Nor is the "phenomenological life" or the "life" of the Absolute Spirit anything but the most questionable extension by metaphor of what any simple culture calls life. Socrates was far more clearheaded when he said right out that the philosophical life is "learning how to die." The justification of reflection by its truth or vital value is inadmissible; it seeks to accredit an activity by the achievement of goals absolutely foreign in essence to it. The inherent home of the good, true, and beautiful is never in reflection, but in precisely those acts of mind upon which reflection reflects and which in our present discussion is called "culture." If "phenomenology" is the current name for the most radical and transcendental reflection, it is no wonder that "existentialism" rises always as its counterpart; phenomenology is the philosophical expression of civilization, and existential thought frequently the reversion to the posture of direct culture by civilized minds. Before the act of civilization men never thought of themselves as "existentialists."

If these civilized motives then are insufficient to answer the question of why men civilized themselves, we are not yet at the end of our resources. Why indeed should the human spirit depart from the "existential," that is, from the direct life of culture? Our answer given above is because the Golden Age is *boring*. But boredom itself should receive some attention, necessary mostly because the moralists regard it as utterly frivolous, itself a product of a worn-out civilization, jaded nerves, a superfluity of the sensuous, something in effect worse than a sin, since boredom is also bored with the category of sin. Baudelaire's greatest offense lay far less in his official vices than in the frankness of his confession of ennui.

What we are looking for is that which lies beneath or is beyond the true, good, and beautiful of the Golden Age, the age of direct life; something in short which is not *wholly* expressed in those values and which therefore offers itself the option of escaping from them. And what could that be but the human spirit itself, defined now as that not wholly given over to the values of culture but given over to something else, given over perhaps to its own life, which is always *activity*. But activity in the present domain is an act of transforming the given. It is, so to speak, the art of the soul. And now, given the spirit, which *is* transformative activity, what would such a spirit *do* in the Garden of Eden, having tasted its direct delights, except escape; and how escape except by that act of reflection upon itself which so profoundly transforms the direct meaning of life itself? Animals fall asleep when nothing moves; equally the immobility of the spirit is its death. The movement open to it is not so much the transformation of its world, planting new gardens or devising new means of irrigation; it is that inner act by which its former reality becomes a phenomenon of its own devising, in a word, the reflection that is the essence of civilization. The spirit must act if it is to live, and the one act by which it can escape asphyxiation by the sincerities of the good, true, and beautiful is to *look* at them, *reflect* upon them, put them within quotation marks so that, having lost their real, direct meanings, they can be *played with*. Civilization now appears as a vast amusement park of no direct value to life, not a culture, indefensible by direct value, and in depth a remedy to the menacing boredom of the spirit. But to preserve the life of the spirit is hardly a frivolous value, even when its works are one and all defined by insincerity, artificiality, and amusement.

Lest this seem far too theoretical, let us take a glance at some phenomena. Civilization, we have said, is the social form of reflection. But what could more foster reflection than an *encounter with others unlike myself?* And where would that occur preeminently except in the city? No wonder that civilization is fundamentally an affair of cities. Cities of course are not large villages, nor is the difference merely quantitative. The city in developed form has a wholly different sense than a village, the one pertaining to civilization, the other to culture. The village is the way families and clans live together, loving its old traditions, its old gods, more or less self-sufficient, and highly suspicious of both strangers and the new. The city on the other hand is unthinkable without its foreigners, slaves, merchants, travelers, its dispossessed and rootless, all of which it now holds together not by custom but by explicit, written law, enforced by magistrates now appointed or elected but decreasingly hereditary. "Justice" is no longer located in the eyes of one's family, measured against all personal loyalties, but something hitherto unique, "equality," namely the equalization of the "rights" of an inherently motley population. The city is the perfect place for rights and duties, the rule of law rather than persons, and all of this culminates in its most active institution, the law court, where words rule supreme.

The spirit of the city offers us the archetypical example of the spirit of civilization. A few years ago in Cambodia, riding in a pedicab outside of Siem Reap through a small garden of Eden, complete with banana trees, a small stream full of fish, and some very young people playing naked in the water, I asked the driver why no young men were to be seen. Only children and grandparents were waving from the thatched huts. "They're bored," he said; "they've all gone off to Siem

Reap where there are bicycles, movies, lights, and the bars."
Was this a mistake? I saw before my eyes the self-expulsion
from the Garden of Eden of young men who could no longer
endure their beautiful lives, even to the point of choosing the
shoddy, backward "city" of Siem Reap. There they would see
movies showing them further excitements . . . . They would
never return home.

The transformation worked by the city touches everything.
What had hitherto been quite natural as dress, manners,
speech, occupation now takes on an ethnic aspect; that is, it
looks local, quaint, primitive, and definitely not modern. It
sinks to a dialectical past, that which has already been
surpassed. It is first a matter of shame, then laughter, then in
the weariness of civilization with itself, it is rediscovered,
imitated, and exhibited. Civilized reflection is always an act of
abstraction from the immediate and concrete; it is necessarily
universal, rational, and international. To reflection, the authority of the traditional disappears and is replaced by the general
law; neither reflection nor reason has any past in itself; the
"past" for reflection is that which is reflected upon, namely,
the life of culture, the instinctive work of mind now to be
understood with rational categories.

The civilized spirit celebrating itself now endeavors to
*manufacture everything,* to remake the old, to invent, to
expose the secret and sacred ways of nature so it can repeat or
modify natural processes at will. Deliberate and methodical
arts supplant magical practices and reverence. Reflection
overcomes the instinctive acts of mind, puts them into its past
and valorizes itself for the first time as the "modern." But the
modern, whatever else it is, is nothing but amusement and
play; the traditional, which is what always was, is the stable
source of that very seriousness reflection flees; the modern in
essence is perpetually changing, can never catch up with itself,
and enjoys this very motion. It can never get stale until one
tires of the category of the modern or until civilization
transcends itself.

If spoken language is the medium of culture, civilization is
dominated by the written word, which seeks to give a
deceptive permanence to the whirl of reflection, to communi-

cate with persons not present, to inform civilized persons of that which they have never experienced. Existentially considered, it is a form of *dislocation:* paper speaking to men in general of things they have never seen. It enlarges consciousness by directing it away from where it is. To the thoroughly if not absurdly civilized man, affairs exist largely in what is written about them, the word displaces the thing, and now the world exists in a new medium where it can be played with at will, all experienced with the exaltation of a freedom from the old and instinctive life where not everything has to be said. In the classical old, high cultures, the king felt no pressing necessity to either read or write; he hired a clerk for the job.

Civilization both is created by and creates its own habitat. The dwelling of the village becomes an apartment, the temporary abode of the restless spirit. Its decor must be changed yearly to ward off tedium and to keep up. Better yet is the trailer, or mobile home, a contradiction in terms to life as lived in a village. The modern spirit is frankly devoted to excitement and entertainment, not surprising since those values were its very origin. The city is full of shows and in all respects is nothing but an enormous showplace for things, people, events. Everything that had its own existential location in village culture is now taken out of context and put on show; what are cities like Florence or Venice but museums of museums? The arts of culture are turned into "aesthetic" objects to be admired for their "composition" since that is all they have left, ripped out of their sacred functions. And so with the great libraries, zoos, and universities where books, animals, and sciences are offered to all. The medium within which such activities are equalized in value is money, which by abstracting from each thing its unique value and essence turns everything into comparable units, a kind of language of the marketplace. In contrast, the New Guinean hesitates to use money; he looks upon each coin as a unique thing, to be prized for itself and its associations and not in the least equal in value to another of the same denomination. They are like shells, each of which is itself. Copper pennies are preferred to silver coins of the same value; copper is more beautiful than pale silver.

It would not be difficult to trace every characteristic phase of civilization back to the same sources, that reflection away from the instincts of mind that form culture. From the shops, shows, restaurants, nightclubs, the buying and selling, the emergence of tourism as a way of life competing with religion, the transformation of marriage into love affairs, the final need for psychoanalysis, sleeping-pills, and liquor before the troubled sleep—all of this was in outline foreseen by Baudelaire with that very ambiguity which characterizes civilization itself. The "sincere," the "bourgeois," the sacrosanct and sanctimonious must give way to the "modern"; and what is that but a kind of bonfire of the free spirit? The fuel is nothing less than the values of instinctive culture, the good, true, and beautiful; the igniting spark is boredom and the promise of amusement; the spectacle itself is neither the truth, nor the beauty, nor the moral value of anything: it is simply the glee of the life of the spirit.

### Excursus: Baudelaire to Duchamp

In his poetry, prose poems, and criticism Baudelaire is the modern civilized man *par excellence*. If others tried to see throughout history a universal type that increasingly began to look like the "common people," Baudelaire celebrated the Dandy, contemptuous of the bourgeoisie, useless, a *flaneur* of Paris, rich, and without obligations beyond amusing himself. If historical painters sought the great scenes of history where universal meanings were highlighted, such as David's "The Death of Socrates," Baudelaire celebrated Constantin Guys, "the painter of modern life," who caught the passing parade, sketched at the battlefront or the racetrack, perceived the eternal in the absolutely ephemeral. If Rubens doted on natural flesh in rosy bloom, Baudelaire scorned it all in favor of "cosmetics"; as for the natural in general, he "refused to worship a row of vegetables." The sumptuous, exotic, savage in a Delacroix were the proper food of the imagination, and then by a final reversal, wholly typical of both Baudelaire and the modern, he also could find "nothing more interesting than the common-place." "The beautiful is always the bizarre," he said somewhat in anticipation of André Breton. If, straightforwardly, good was to be loved and evil hated in an eternal opposition, for Baudelaire evil grew its own unique flowers.

If Baudelaire was one of the first and last *celebrants* of the peculiarly modern, Marcel Duchamp passes beyond, both to help create and at the same time to exhaust the delights of Dada, surely the final phase of civilization beyond which there is only backtracking. If the "serious" painters, like Cézanne and Picasso, work into old age furiously battling with the problems of making an oil painting, Duchamp after some early triumphs such as the *Nude Descending the Staircase* became bored with canvas and oil paint, worked some seven years on a glass, *The Bride Stripped Bare By Her Bachelors, Even*, where love was reduced to a curious machine constructed not in accordance with physics but Duchamp's own physics of chance, a kind of pataphysics. But then he got bored with that too and it remains definitively unfinished. There were other serious amusements such as his ready-mades, where snow shovels, bicycle wheels mounted on kitchen chairs, retouched cheap lithos, or combs were presented to the art world as objects of interest. This too became boring, so Duchamp amused himself with chess, only to become bored with that. "What do you do now," he was once asked: "I breathe," he replied, implying a kind of *euphoria* in his "meta-irony." With Pierre Cabanne° he expresses again and again his "motive": "it was amusing," along with, "I have always been lazy." Art was a "drug" from which he had long ago cured himself.† In a superb picture of the old master we see the final face of civilization.‡ He has seen through that too.

## Götterdämmerung

Culture passes into civilization, but that magnificent auto-da-fé of the free spirit cannot possibly burn out of its own resources since it has none. It lasts only so long as there is a

---

° *Dialogues with Marcel Duchamp* (London: Thames and Hudson, 1971).

† Calvin Tomkins, ed., *The World of Marcel Duchamp* (New York: Time Inc., 1966), p. 173.

‡ Though not completely or without some nostalgia, as the last work at the Philadelphia Museum shows.

trace of the naive life of mind left to burn up. What then is the dialectical or dramatic future of civilization so conceived?

Three possibilities are open, a reversion to its past, that is, the endeavor to create a new primitive culture; the persistence in its own present through variations on its themes; or the passage into its future, which carries it beyond civilization into something else altogether.

The temptation toward a reversion back to the stage of a relatively primitive culture is always great, particularly so in mass civilizations like those of modern times. Obviously never more than a small proportion of men in any high civilization really are civilized or reap in any authentic fashion the benefits of civilization. In effect they live out their lives more or less as butts of jokes or as the objects of scorn by the aristocracy of the civilization. They are the "middle classes," the "bourgeoi-sie," half-educated, rising by newly acquired wealth alone, and avid purchasers of books and works of art whose chief content is the ridicule of themselves, with which they share a chuckle too. But it is all half-understood, and when one reflects that the aristocrats of civilization *also* frequently enjoy economic privileges, what can the finally enraged and disappointed ones do but dismantle the existing civilization in favor of a new "people's culture," one that can be "shared by all"? The new culture, not surprisingly, is always held to be "more natural" than the now hated civilization, perceived as a life-stifling artificiality. The sanctification of agriculture and hand labor is quick to follow, education is made more practical, and men of the people have an advantage in politics. Foreign languages become an affectation, passports for traveling become more difficult to get, disloyalty to the new state culture is increas-ingly scrutinized. For "thought" the meditations of the Leader are not merely sufficient, but anything beyond is somewhat suspect. These "thoughts," whether from *Mein Kampf* or the *Little Red Book* are to be committed to memory and chanted on public occasions; they are not subject to scrutiny, let alone laughter. These new primitive cultures all prize "sincerity," that is, a peculiar form of humorlessness, against which the older civilization is judged to be sickened with hypocrisy, salon wit, arrogance, hauteur, frivolity, degeneration, and internationalism. It is not long before the Jews, as internationalists *par excellence,* begin to feel the folk pressure.

Civilization is always susceptible to this internal disintegration back into an artificially generated new culture. Nor can it be surprising to the dialectician of history to see each new culture, if it is given a long enough life, proceed to civilize itself back into what it had just despised. The new culture begins to laugh at itself, to crave leisure, to relax the revolutionary morality, to be just a little wicked; and soon, bored stiff with the people's earnest values of the good, true, and beautiful, it debauches itself back into the cynical laughter of civilization. This particular cycle, always at the cost of tens of thousands of lives, looks too much like the bad or repetitive infinite of Hegel.

The second path open to the civilized spirit is, of course, to go on with the infinite variations possible to it. After all, it can always improve itself with educational, economic, or political reforms. And the arts have a way of becoming their own subject matter, such that this year's works are commentaries upon last year's. There will always be a new generation, alienated from what is, ready to make it all new. Since the turning of this glittering wheel offers us nothing essentially new, we shall pass it by to examine the third alternative. After all, the dialectical future of civilization is not yet another civilization.

## Beyond Civilization

The same intrinsic motive that generated civilization out of naive culture, boredom, also serves to propel it out of civilization itself; what indeed could be more boring than the perpetual artificiality, invention, and restlessness of the civilized life? Wit tires of wit, the gourmet no longer seeks the new dish, love has twisted and turned through too many affairs, and the arts end up mocking themselves. The civilized mind either longs to extinguish civilization altogether into a new culture, or else, foreseeing the eventual civilizing of that too, looks elsewhere; but where else is there?

Culture lives in the village, civilization in cities; where else can the spirit now live except within its own privacy? The form of life, then, that carries the spirit beyond civilization will not be essentially social, by which it is not meant that "cities will disappear" historically. They may very well, but that is hardly our question. Our question touches rather the possibility of a withdrawal of primary interest in the business and work of civilization into a *final* interest, the recovery of the human spirit by itself. For *this* work there is no social form; it must be the work of the individual with other individuals perhaps, in personal communication. But even then the transcendental solitude of the spirit can never be abrogated by itself or breached by another without a defeat of its project.

This project of the spirit, to recall and recover itself, we shall call, following Hegel, "absolute." From this standpoint culture is the instinctive, dreaming life of mind; civilization represents the reflection upon that dreaming life, promoted by the other person. The face of each expresses his response to what he sees in the face of the other, looking at him. The face of civilization, then, is inherently bland, tired, the mirror of a mirror. The possible person has been dissipated into the other, who in turn is dissipated into his other. Both culture and civilization are "one-sided"; and the question is raised whether the spirit cannot recover itself not by regression but by development. The recovery of the spirit by itself is not an obliteration of its previous development but an understanding of its one-sidedness through perhaps a new perception of itself. As no longer one-sided, it may be called "absolute"; is there a further development that it can perceive?

The inherent work is now that of living mind and not another social product of civilization. Nevertheless, such personal work finds its way into civilization as an expression in the arts, religion, and philosophy. For traces of that work, then, we shall look at some contemporary expressions in these three domains: surrealism, existential religion, and transcendental philosophy.

### SURREALISM

Surrealism from the first had a marked preference for the "primitive." A "surrealist map of the world" shows an

enormously enlarged New Guinea and an enormously
shrunken United States and Europe. New Guinea, Africa, the
Easter Islands, the Hopi Indians, these were the last bastions
of the old culture untouched by civilization. Moreover, the
primitive in each man was to be released, that domain ruined
by reason, science, self-consciousness, and their delusive sense
of reality. At first glance then surrealism might appear to be a
regressive stage; and yet a closer look shows the opposite. The
surrealists did not wish to *become* primitives, except in some
wilder moments, and, while they prized the minds of the child,
the insane, and the criminal, they themselves remained for the
most part under control. In fact what was cultivated was a
double or paradoxical consciousness of both the real and the
unreal. The surreal they sought and expressed always bore an
indirect reference to the reality it was above. Breton in the
*First Manifesto* says: "I believe in the future resolution of these
two states, dream and reality . . . into a kind of absolute
reality, a surreality." And again in the *Second Manifesto*:
"Everything tends to make us believe that there exists a
certain point of mind at which life and death, the real and the
imagined, past and future, the communicable and the incommunicable, high and low cease to be perceived as contradictions." * The affinity of this "point of mind" with Hegel's
Absolute is obvious and explicitly recognized by Breton. Its
affinities with the mystical works of Ekhardt and the "coincidentia oppositorum" of Cusanus need not be belabored. For
our present purposes it may be enough to remark that,
historically developing out of dadaism, surrealism offers what
is already beyond civilization, an effort at an absolute recuperation of the spirit, but not on the plane of reason, reflection, or
civilization, all of which now pass as one element into a new
final synthesis. And it is not surprising that surrealism is not
merely an aesthetic but a form of life aimed at "freedom,
poetry, and mad love." Its politics were usually revolutionary,
and its social form consisted of small groups, with shifting
membership and weekly meetings, that became increasingly

* André Breton, *Manifestoes of Surrealism*, trans. Seaver and Lane (Ann Arbor:
University of Michigan Press, 1969), pp. 14 and 123.

exclusive. It entered the civilized world mostly in the form of outrageous demonstrations and exhibitions; its proper life was its own.

## EXISTENTIAL RELIGIONS

Beyond civilization are also certain religious directions, many of which originated with Kierkegaard. Characteristic is the violent anticlericalism expressed in Kierkegaard's *The Instant*, where official priests are declared to be worse than murderers and the whole of official Christianity, with its concomitant notion of a "Christian civilization," is excoriated as an enormous fraud. And all in the name not of a new church or new civilization, but of *inwardness*, an absolute and solitary living in the presence of an Absolute Telos, God. It is absolute, and if *anything* in the world should stand in the way, it must be discarded. Abraham, in *Fear and Trembling*, provides the archetypical example of both the absoluteness of his devotion to God and the essential incommunicability of that faith. He may give an example to those who can understand but his work does not consist essentially in improving upon civilization or founding a new one. That inwardness may as well be called ontological autobiography.

## TRANSCENDENTAL PHILOSOPHY

Philosophy as a function of civilization is a "rational," "teachable" enterprise, more or less summed up as "analysis." Analysis of what, except the direct, naive, or instinctive acts of mind and speech. In its analytical role it is essentially piecemeal, looking now at this, now at that, eschewing by both taste and method anything aiming at the synthetic or systematic. Analysis is self-multiplying by a form of spiritual parthenogenesis: the analysis is no sooner given than it too invites further analysis, which in turn . . . all of which gives us a perfect image of the hidden intentions defining civilization by its interminable reflection. And yet if recollection of the spirit is sought, what used to be called "wisdom" in those parts of the philosophical classics that are no longer read or taught, it can hardly be found through any extension of analytical reflection. And so we now hasten over those parts of Plato where the philosopher is considered to be the "spectator of all time and existence." Could anything be more pretentious, less teachable?

And yet happily there are and always have been signs that philosophers recuperate themselves from time to time, take up their personal and private-task of understanding the life of the mind, even when they decide it is not understandable. The work of understanding must of course be the work of the philosophic self and not a group engaged in what they might imagine to be a collective "scientific" project. It remains the act of that self no matter how many sympathizers form a "school" around it. It may be expressed, but then the purport of the expression could hardly be to compel any exclusive assent to what is said; it resembles a conceptual confession, which from time to time also uses arguments. It does not seek to generate a new civilization unless it misunderstands itself. But unless it seeks some final and transcendental understanding of itself as philosophy and of the existence of the living person of the philosopher, it has not risen above the controversies of the schools. Where it does aim at such understanding, it represents an effort to achieve something that can no longer be a part of civilization but looks at that absolute point where life and death are one, which has one foot in life and another outside, and where perhaps the spirit can recuperate itself by understanding how it itself arose, and where its final destiny lies: always with itself.

*Part 2*

# PRIVATE PLEASURES: PHILOSOPHY

# Seven

◇◇◇

# *Art as Philosophy*

PHILOSOPHERS and artists have, since the beginning, always been uneasy in one another's company. For, while each aimed at the highest, each also suspected the other of some merit denied himself. Plato, according to legend, began as a dramatist but he met Socrates and tore up his plays, only to emerge again as a philosophical dramatist, where the conflict of passion and interest was transmuted into that of opposed theories. In the absence of the original plays, it is hard to judge whether this was an improvement or not. But from then on, insofar as a distinction was recognized between philosophy and art, philosophy was determined by the philosopher to be the winner. The philosopher could perceive the Real through the eye of reason alone; the artist was confined to making questionable imitations three removes from that reality. Knowing the Good, the philosopher was ideally destined to rule the state and guard its virtue and justice; the artist, on the contrary seemingly devoted to pleasure, was irresponsible, was a creator of poems that excited immoral or ungovernable passions, and worse, was careless of their effect. The philosopher could defend himself in argument, but the artist, knowing nothing of dialectic and definitions, substituted rhetoric and the charms of the imagination. Naturally he cut a poor figure indeed in argument. The philosopher could do by rule and reason what, at best, the poet did by gifts, inspiration, and a certain interior disorder. His greatest hope in his own unreliable and dangerous way was, as an illusionist, to touch off occasionally and unbeknownst to himself a deep truth, certifiable by the philosopher.

For Aristotle, while the scene changes radically, poetry remains a second-best thing; it is higher than history, for while history only tells us what was, poetry makes it probable; but science and philosophy win the day eventually, for they succeed in grasping the *necessary*.

Without retracing the history of philosophy, we see clearly that from the start philosophy took a keen interest in its rival, art; and it developed a variety of disciplines reflecting philosophically upon the arts, all lumped together here as "aesthetics" or the "philosophy *of* art." The arts are examined and compared with other activities and objects, with regard to their natures, powers, origins, and effects moral and otherwise. Now, no doubt at all, something can be said under each of these heads; but in sum it all remains a philosophical rather than artistic performance, with philosophical rather than aesthetic ideals in mind. Even for Hegel, one of the last great aestheticians, while art could indeed express Absolute Spirit, alas it did so only in the medium of the imagination, and its final truth must be grasped by the philosophical idea. What is striking throughout is that the philosophy of art is itself three times removed from its proper subject matter; the work itself is primary; its critical interpretation comes next; and at last the philosophy of art works upon the deliverances of criticism.

Now some, feeling perhaps that the artist was being given a bum rap by the philosopher, attempted a closer *rapprochement* in the form of "philosophy *in* the arts." From Santayana's beautiful *Three Philosophical Poets*, through innumerable critical studies such as Sullivan's on Beethoven, down to the latest college course in the subject, the philosopher now looks for philosophical meanings in the arts, most usually of course literature. And yet there is something profoundly disturbing about these efforts; what is it that the philosopher will recognize as "philosophical"? It will of course be some general statement expressing an attitude toward life, whether tragic or comic, about the condition of men, either always or just now, in a word, some contributions to a general philosophical theory of man, life, or recently even Being. Critics of an ethical cast of mind have a field day, since any human behavior can be thought of as having an ethical dimension; some have even supposed the artist to have ethical theories, but those theories are far more explicit in the correspondence or conversation of the artist than in his works. Again, one perceives the perpetual discomfort of fundamentally abstract minds confronting the dismayingly concrete and singular. In this vein "to be or not to be" is thought to be "philosophical," while "my horse, my horse, my kingdom for a horse" is mere filler. Unquestionably such philosophers can frequently produce works of considerably higher value than some mediocre work of art upon which they are based; but the distance between the work and what is said of it remains infinite. The plot must be reduced to a skeleton; the characters are understood under general rubrics; and in the end we are left with a handful of conceptual banalities as the philosophy in the work. The work itself has long been forgotten or, worse, transformed into a preliminary pedagogical device to convey truths hardly worth mentioning.

So far, then, we have two attempts to relate philosophy and art: art as a subject matter for philosophy, or art as embalming some general philosophical truths. The rest of the chapter will develop the remaining possibility, neither the philosophy *of* art of which this essay is itself an example, nor philosophy *in* the arts, but rather philosophy as art, or, better, art *as* philosophy. And, to state my conclusions at once, they mean to affirm that works of art actually accomplish what philosophy only hopes to do, that art is therefore philosophy perfected. The tables should therefore be turned: philosophy even on its own criteria can be justified only insofar as it offers a concrete imaginative intuition measureable against those for which the arts are famous. And for this reversal, surprisingly, we might even share the company of some philosophers themselves, those as otherwise diverse as Schelling, Schopenhauer, Bergson, and Croce.

To defend this reversal I should first like to examine the medium of philosophical and scientific thought, and then the purpose to which the medium is put. As for the medium, philosophy, whatever else it is thought to be, offers itself as knowledge, and knowledge of a distinctive sort. It is, briefly, *conceptual, propositional,* and *argued.* A philosopher who lacked concepts or propositional theses or, worse, who spoke without argument, not to say wrangling, would be reclassified by the dean, as well as his colleagues. But this medium of discursive thought is put to some distinctive purpose: the philosopher hopes to know something final, comprehensive, and ultimately true, not just any little thing. Let us look at both the instruments of knowledge and its purpose in turn.

First the *concept.* Obviously not any mode of apprehending something is conceptual. The concept or the idea is a distinctive mode of apprehending things, and what it apprehends of things is equally distinctive. To *look* at a man, accordingly, is *not yet* to *think* him in the form of a concept, or example of a concept. It is simply to apprehend a singular individual. Perception, memory, imagination all share this particular feature, to wit, they are modes of apprehending singular things and their singular activities, and therefore can be called modes of "intuition." The concept is therefore something distinct from intuition, and Kant contrasted them in his famous remark: "Concepts without intuitions are empty, intuitions without concepts are blind." Only their marriage was productive of knowledge; yet there is room for a skeptic to doubt the fruitfulness of a marriage between blindness and emptiness. And if the concept is indeed empty, is intuition blind? But intuition in the first place is a mode of apprehending; to intuit, to see, imagine, remember, is precisely to apprehend *something,* and a "blind intuition" is as good as none at all, nor does it need the empty concept superadded to it in order to perform that which it does in its own right quite adequately, namely, to see something.

If, then, it is obvious that intuition in any of its modes does indeed offer us an apprehension of something and not nothing, what on earth does the "concept," or idea of that thing already apprehended intuitively, *add?* Traditionally it is taken as adding the dimension of *universality,* and I have no reason to quarrel with this interpretation. If intuitively I see a man, I do not yet have a concept of him. If I then form an idea or concept of him, "humanity," I have abstracted from the singular presentation, this man, that which is of universal coverage, humanity. Humanity is, then, what the concept apprehends of this man by noticing in the singular object only that which *could* be predicated of other singulars. It should be noticed that the universal is achieved by an act of omission or, as Kant had it, "emptying." I empty from my mind all that which individuates this man from that man, or, which is the same, I abstract from the singular or refuse to notice that in the singular which singularizes this man from that. And it should be noticed, Hume to the contrary notwithstanding, that what is now left before the mind is not a faint image of this man, or a composite photograph of all the men I have seen or heard about, but a new object altogether, a concept, which can be understood as an ideal entity accompanied by a rule for its exemplification. The new ideal entity, while not an image, is related to intuition by way of omission and formalization. It omits everything not duplicable in the intuition, and transforms it thereby into a universal form. The conceptualization of the world therefore adds not a whit to it, restricts its attention to its duplicable features, and formalizes it. Now this is essential to any philosophy that aims at universal statements; but since it is a *subtractive* mode of apprehension, it must from the concrete aesthetic standpoint be regarded as a radical impoverishment of what is available. What is already available is the intuited concrete, with both its singular and unique aspects, as well as its capability of being formalized, if anyone should wish to do so. In a word, we have Hamlet, and not Man, nor *a* prince of Denmark but this singular caught in his singular situation, making his singular decisions, and suffering his singular death. Now while any of this *could* serve as an example of precisely that universal of which it is an example, it is hard to see to what profit. The singular unrepeatable aspects of singular lives are what the arts are admirably equipped to show; what might be called the "existential"; the conceptualization of the existential is but a questionable flight from it, one which moreover can only be proven correct or incorrect by a return precisely to that intuited from which it took its flight. The possession of the concept or definition was much prized from antiquity on; it gave the philosopher eyes to see beyond the immediate, into the timeless, placeless beyond; this was his "higher truth." Plato expresses admiration for Thales, for falling into a well while looking beyond at the stars. But if the concept can indeed blind us to what lies before our feet, what it offers, if not exactly stars, could be nothing but what we already see, turned into what we do not, in a word, an existential disorientation.

But concepts are designed to be elements of propositions. Science and philosophy therefore pride themselves upon their ability to make assertions that are either true or false; and, as tradition has it, neither concepts by themselves nor intuition by itself can make an assertion. Hence they are not *true*, since truth resides in propositional judgment or statement. To see a man is certainly not the same thing as to form the judgment "that is a man." And it follows at once that the truths of science and philosophy cannot be painted, narrated, or played upon our violins. And it is supposed to follow that what is played upon the violin, since it makes no assertion that is true or false, has no serious relation to truth. But perhaps this should be reexamined. I shall use the terms "judgment" and "proposition" here as more or less interchangeable.

The judgment or proposition, like the concept, is a distinctive mode of thinking, so distinctive that perhaps it escapes our attention how rarely we form any such thing. The judgment aims at saying something true about its purported subject. It is not an exclamation, invitation, or expression of subjective feeling, but an assertion that something objectively independent of either me or my judgment is such-and-such. It is a declaration about something or other which is as it is independently of my judgment. The judgment says, "It is so." No mere experience says of itself, "It *is* so." It just shows something as so. On the other hand, Beethoven, who doubtless never heard of this distinction, didn't hesitate to write a quartet, in which the music was to go from "must it be" to "it must be," although at the present point it could be argued that even this much must be said in words; or was it also in the music? If truth resides in the proposition or judgment, what *sort* of truth is it whose exclusive home is there? Is truth to be denied to the arts by virtue of the fact that in their capacity of showing us something they refrain from the propositional judgment *that* it is so, let alone of offering us the opportunity of verifying any such judgment?

The *declarative judgment,* in which truth is supposed to reside, is inherently *objective.* By that I mean that the proposition declares that what it proposes is true of something independent of the proposition, some fact. The proposition is not true in and of itself, but *of* something else, and by virtue of an external relation usually called "correspondence." Hence no inspection of the meaning of the proposition will be sufficient to determine whether independent fact is what the proposition says it is. I am referring here obviously to what are called "synthetic, a posteriori" propositions, that is, propositions about the contingent features of the world. Analytic propositions, which seem to be true by definition or which simply explicate the meanings of the concepts composing them, are not propositions in this sense; at very least they raise the question whether they are about anything at all independent of the meanings involved. Whether they are also true of independent reality in its necessary features is a question we can leave aside; I believe it to be the case, but to argue the matter here would be to no particular present point. In any event, analytic propositions do not require empirical verification, and do not express contingent or factual features of an independent reality. The mathematician performs no experiments or observations, and contents himself with the phenomenon of internal meanings. Whether his truths are true of everything or nothing we shall leave open for the present.

Ordinary factual propositions that purport to be true, then, are true of something else, something independent and objective. Further, the declarative proposition makes its declaration *to* a peculiar aspect of ourselves, in effect, to some "anybody" in each of us, what the Germans call *Bewusstsein überhaupt,* that aspect of the thinking mind which, being exclusively directed to the truth of objective reality, is neither me nor you, but a logical function in which we share equivalent and replaceable roles. For Kant it was the transcendental unity of apperception, or for Husserl, the Transcendental Ego. Hence declarative propositions, if they are true at all, are true *for everybody;* their truth is measured against the fact, and not myself, my feelings, my life. For either a mathematician or a chemist to say that something was true for him and him alone would be for him to confess that he had not yet achieved an objective truth, and that instead he was confessing something about himself, perhaps nothing more than a hunch that his proposition was true. Science is objective in two senses: it is about an independent fact, and it is true for everyone, whether he likes it or not.

If soem such thing is how it stands with propositional truth, have we not already precluded the arts as a proper medium of it? To restrict ourselves now to the verbal arts, surely no poem makes any declarative statement about an *independent reality* whose truth must be *compelling* upon *absolutely* everybody. Although using historical materials for allusion, the play *Hamlet* most certainly does not make declarative statements about the independent historical Prince of Denmark, about whom relatively little is known, and of whom no one bothers to think while watching the play. And while Proust's *Remembrance of Things Past* is set in the early twentieth century, and is a fascinating source of clues and gossip about this or that historical character, it can and is easily read not as historical memoirs of the period, but as a work of art in which no character, including the narrator, ever lived or felt in precisely that way. It's all "as if" memoirs, and so works may be historical or autobiographical in origin, setting, allusion; but it is exactly the transformation of those facts into the work which constitutes the art of the artist. Therefore, in experiencing the work we are far more like mathematicians engrossed in our own definitions and meanings than empirical scientists checking what is said against a reality available to us otherwise. There is *no* independent reality against which the work of art is checked for its truth; and in effect we are in a quandary just like mathematicians or logicians as to whether the word "truth" is applicable any more. *About what* are these works true?

The sentence in a work of literature surely never has the function of making a declarative assertion about facts that could be checked otherwise. On the contrary they are expressions not certainly of the artist, but of the content of the sentence itself. They bring to expression their own intuitional content, and do it in the clearest possible way. Compositions of sentences are compositions of intuitions, and the whole rings true when the whole is faithful to its parts, or is indeed the whole of those parts and no others. What Hamlet does is true to his character established that far; his character is true equivalently to what he does. The truth, then, of works of art is internal to them, or equivalent to their internal coherence. They share this ideal with logic and dialectic. The work is true to itself when it achieves not the artist's personal aim, but the embodied aim of the work, which is to show or express some concrete imaginative reality to us. And since concrete reality is *necessarily* surprising, the ideal of coherence must not be taken as excluding it. Concrete, imaginative reality would be surprising indeed if it were not surprising. It would therefore be false to the singular individuals presented to us in literature if we considered them solely as puppets of some abstract ideas. Since that is not what they are presented as, to show them so would be an internal inconsistency, false in itself.

If the demonstrative proposition addresses itself to reason or to the universal thinker in each of us, the intuitive, expressive sentence does not. I think this point will become clear if we consider the sentence "Caesar crossed the Rubicon" as it might occur in a work of history, and as it might occur in a poem. In the work of history our attention passes through the sentence to the fact it describes and proposes. Neither the person of the reader nor the particular formation or quality of the sentence is at issue. The sentence serves as an instrument to point to something else. But the same sentence as it might occur expressively in a poem does not invite us to think of anything but what it presents and how it is presented. Further, while the barest experience would be sufficient to understand declarative sentences, when, in fact, the same content is offered to us for our intuition, it makes an appeal to the whole of our experience to render up that intuition itself. And consequently the reader of the poem is far more deeply and personally involved than the anonymous and replaceable reader of declarative sentences, no matter how complex they are.

The net result of which is that the declarative, propositional medium of philosophy is inherently *disruptive* of whatever unity or coherence truth might have. If the poem invites a unity of reader, work, and content such that at best they are hardly experienced as distinct, the medium of philosophy and science, the declarative sentence, demands a distinction between thinker, his thinking, and what is thought of—in brief, a built-in schizophrenia. And further, since these three can only be *accidentally* related, the kind of truth aimed at propositionally is an accidental, externally related composition which, when the worst is said, can hardly be of any value except that of expediency in life.

At this point we can be briefer about the third claim of the philosophical medium, to wit, that it at least can *prove* its propositional claims, while the helpless arts can at best show truth without proof or argument. The classic remark of Laplace upon seeing Racine, *"Qu'est que ça prouve?"* may be taken as archetypical. And let us agree that while in literary works of art we may find arguments within, when one character argues with another or with the gods or with himself, the whole taken as a work of art never argues that it itself is indeed true of anything, except on pain of changing its genre into history or science.

Why do philosophers argue? Charity forbids answering: to prove *themselves* right; we shall say: to prove a proposition true. True, that is, of an independent reality. Classically, propositions are either true in themselves, that is, self-evident, or proven true through other propositions, or proven true by consulting the contingent world in experience. Let us for convenience omit self-evident propositions; while I believe there are such, and that they need no further argument, still to argue *that* is already to put ourselves under other criteria. If propositions are proven true through other propositions, then we achieve that form of truth manifest in coherence, now the coherence of propositions. In demonstration, premises yield coherent conclusions. In dialectic, obscure or misstated propositions are developed into clearer or more coherent propositions by forcing the earlier into contradictions, later cleared up. Both of these forms of construction, demonstration, and dialectic are obviously directed toward coherence of meaning and propositional statement. So considered, none of the arts can offer anything comparable. But then, why should they? They needn't prove anything about anything else, since they are not about anything else, and thus under no such obligation. Presenting their own unique reality in person, they can be blessedly free from anything to be superadded in the form of a proof. If philosophy could indeed *show* its own proper subject matter, would there ever be an occasion for proof? And so, instead of a merit, the need for proof must be considered an inherent fault, the consequences philosophy reaps for having abandoned reality in the first place via the concept. It all comes to a head with those miserable *synthetic a posteriori* propositions, always about the contingent factual world. True, philosophy isn't even much interested in any one of them, although the theory of them in general occupies many. They preeminently are about the external world; and, as is notorious and obvious, they must all be confirmed by reverting to experience or intuition, helped out in some cases by empirical "laws," themselves but summaries of more general experience.

Finally, to conclude, if such is its medium, what is philosophy's end? *There* might be one point in its favor, namely, that it is invariably *about* ultimate things. Its aim is the Good, the One, God, Being-in-Itself, Absolute Mind, or today, abandoning these high subjects, at least about method or language, a surrogate absolute. One mark of such topics is that no matter how these ultimate things are conceived or alluded to, they have the general character of being *transcendental*, as Kant put it. They constitute in general the *presuppositions* of some domain of experience: ethical acts, meaningful statements, acts of knowledge, or anything at all. Now in their transcendental aspect, they at once remove themselves from the domain of the experienceable, and therewith, it might seem, from the domain of the arts. How could the arts, which succeed by expressing and showing, have anything to do with what in principle never shows itself but is always the presupposition of what does?

In other words, in the last analysis are the arts not engaged in a somewhat frivolous project of merely telling their own miserable little tales, showing visual compositions, playing tunes, and indeed what do these have to do with the serious concerns of metaphysics or theology? And let us throw out at once those allegorical works of literature or painting which *directly name* the transcendent, which either name or show us something called God, Mankind, Life, or even Being, in the person of some actor or chorus—the crucifixions, moral fables, nonobjective paintings of Being, etc., as well as the manifestos and confessions of the artists themselves which, superadded to the work, give us its "real meaning," evidently not sufficiently present in the work itself. All of that may well have other values, but it is not what concerns us here.

What does concern us is the question whether the transcendental concerns of metaphysics or theology can be adequately expressed by artistic shows; or, rather, whether they *can be approached in any other way*. And that question depends on how the ultimate concerns of philosophy are understood. This obviously is no place to attempt to sketch out anything new, nor do I have anything new to say. But, if I may allude to some historical philosophies with which I have moreover great sympathy, at least the outline of a solution might be made visible. The ultimate concerns of philosophy have received a number of names: with Plato, the Good; with Aristotle, Thought thinking thought; God throughout much of the Western middle ages; Substance with Spinoza, Absolute Spirit with Hegel, and perhaps this is enough to indicate some directions, without carrying it into more contemporary and controversial times. Now with such an array of conceptions, conceptions moreover that are not in the least identical, at least a few things are clear: either each names an entity individually distinct from the intuitable world and its things, or not. And, following Hegel's formulations at this point, if the particular philosophy's development considers that ultimate and transcendental presupposition as an entity, distinct from the world, it has at the same stroke turned its own viewpoint upside down; it simply has grasped of the Transcendental Presupposition, yet another individual entity. With that reversal, the transcendental term loses its presuppositional, grounding function and merely sinks to the level of a new and odd thing. Philosophically considered, we might consider it a category mistake; religiously considered, it is superstition and even blasphemy; aesthetically considered, it turns art into empty allegory and bombast. And so, if art looks impoverished at first glance by offering us merely the intuitable, philosophy when it retains its purity is in the same boat; philosophy cannot conceptualize the transcendental preconditions of the concept.

And so the transcendental in philosophy is badly conceived as another particular entity, an entity which has a peculiar ontological status, a name, and for which there is a direct cognitive or demonstrative access. Hence the extremely problematical character of such names as "the transcendent," or questions as to whether "it" exists. No matter how much we talk, the ultimate truths or insights of philosophers remain unsayable.

And now the question remains whether the arts do not preserve a far more reasonable *tact* on these questions. Instead of *proving* that man, his language, his ethical and political concerns, his birth and death are all strange, and with that demonstration secretly destroying the strangeness, the arts show it. The curtain goes up, and we are invited to a spectacle not of Being, Man, Nature, or whatnot, but what all these concretely culminate in, individuals in action. The action is begun and ended with curtains, and we are not asked to intervene, criticize, or do anything but watch. The invitation simply to see without moral or other judgment is at the same time a request to occupy that transcendental standpoint philosophers have themselves always encouraged, to the extent that for Spinoza, philosophical blessedness began with considering men impersonally, precisely as lines, planes, and solids within nature. And if the phenomenologists want to see above all the pure phenomenon without presuppositions and doubtful beliefs, and if they ever should weary of repeating the phenomenology of perception, what better to perceive than the phenomena of ourselves; and who have done it better than the poets?

In a word, the concept is not necessary to see, intuition does it in a far richer way. The declarative proposition is not necessary for truth, but only for a limited form of it. The demonstration or proof may be necessary for empirical truths, but those truths have only the value of practical expedients. The logical medium of philosophy is dispensable for philosophy's own aims which, in the long run, are identical with those of art: to see what *is* from a transcendental standpoint, but that means *seeing,* and for that purpose I believe the arts win the day.

# Eight

◇◇◇

# *Surrealism as Philosophy*

The flora and fauna of surrealism are inadmissible.
I believe in the future resolution of these two states, dream and reality . . . into a kind of absolute reality, a surreality.

*1st Manifesto*

Everything tends to make us believe that there exists a certain point of the mind at which life and death, the real and the imagined, past and future, the communicable and the incommunicable, high and low cease to be perceived as contradictions.

*2nd Manifesto*
André Breton

PHILOSOPHY in the form of metaphysics has, of course, from its first recognizable examples been interested in *what is*, reality. Philosophers have disputed the general character of the real, and whether any candidate for the title of reality deserved it; but the dispute only confirms that the historical intention of metaphysics has aimed at something called reality, and its kinds, to such an extent that it goes without saying. Some philosophers have divided reality into kinds by some dialectical principle: *negation*, as in Being and Nonbeing; *dependence*, as in Substance and its modes; *knowability*, as in noumena and phenomena. These procedures have the advantage that they are completable; a dialectical division exhausts its universe of discourse. But they have the corresponding disadvantage of comprising within one leg of the division what on other grounds would proliferate into the endless. If Being and

Nonbeing exhaust the universe of discourse, it is only because
we have included under one or the other term an infinite
positive diversity. While pencil and not-pencil together name
whatever could be, not-pencil itself comprises an infinity of
forms, now named only by what they are not. Dialectical
divisions of such a sort are easily made; in an instant we
succeed in saying something about everything, but the ease of
such intellectual acts should warn us of their intrinsic poverty.
A humbler but more promising ontology finds itself in an
infinite sea of being, and now must look to see what there is,
with no hope or aspiration of cataloguing it all. Here
empiricism comes into its rights, as well as phenomenology;
neither is interested in dialectical schemes of everything, but
both are content to consult what we *experience*.

In contrast to dialectical or a priori schemata, the reversion
to experience can acquaint us with what we could not have
otherwise predicted, therefore with something fresh. But so far
as I can see, the reversion to experience had had an extremely
unfortunate result, in principle unnecessary and accidental,
but unfortunate nonetheless. The reversion to the evidence of
experience has, in practice, meant the return to *sense perception* as the fundamental mode of consciousness through which
we can become acquainted with the real. The term "experience" itself has become virtually synonomous with sense
perception, and correspondingly the secret prejudice makes
itself known that *the real* in its honorific sense is what is
experienceable by our senses. Now anyone can stipulate any
word to mean anything he likes; there is no quarrel there. But
if the "real" names the ancient aspiration of philosophy, the
very heart of the philosophic enterprise, perhaps the term
"real" should not be so quickly finished off with experience.
The implicit closure of the eternal problem of reality by
confining it to what is experienceable is the disastrous
consequence of a hardly conscious assumption that "experience" of course means sense experience, rather than being the
title for another mystery, consciousness itself.

The net effect of this prejudice in favor of sense perception
is an informal metaphysics of the correlates of sensation, and
an understanding that gets both its materials and its final goals

from the world of sense perception, all now understood to be reality. Reality, once the name of a mystery, is now "understood" to be the perceptible; our so-called epistemologies are the epistemologies of how the perceptible is perceived and how it is to be understood. Dominating all this is a picture that only has to be sketched to exhibit its naiveté. There are things and their properties (or *not:* events); these events or things are bound together by causal laws, not necessarily known, but hoped for; all of this is capable of being grounded in publicly verifiable assertions. Common sense illustrates it informally; but empirical philosophers' notions of science illustrate it even better. The whole enterprise, which began with high hopes and brave promises, ends in a depressing mess of common sense; the direct theme of philosophy now is the old world of things, more or less permanent, events usually thought of as *motions,* the laws that one hopes govern all these things and their events, and the whole world of such banalities, insofar and only insofar as it is publicly accessible. Now there can be no doubt at all that such a version of the old mystical term "reality" has its own clarity, its own logic, makes no demands on the imagination whatsoever, and is some sort or other of what anyone could know without much trouble at all. It is, therefore, eminently *teachable;* perhaps the only teachable version of truth. It even has answers to its problems! And it even conceives a philosophical problem as that which *can* with sufficient application or cleverness be *solved!*

What else is there? Well, since we are located on the plane not of dialectical, a priori, or abstract reason, but *concrete* or *intuitive consciousness,* that is, the immediate consciousness of a particular before it, we might begin to ask whether such consciousness of particular being is confined to sense perception or "experience" so understood. If we choose to remain in the domain of the particular and concrete, is our only acquaintance with it through sense perception? But of course we have forgotten imagination; and it is the surrealists who will not allow us to forget it. The empiricists of ontology say the imagination presents us with what is not real but "only" imaginary; hence it is of no help in our quest for the real. Such is the empirical response. And thus the issues are drawn.

Phenomenology always prided itself on its "presupposition-less" character; it would begin with whatever presented itself to consciousness without prejudging its essence or its mode of being. Each was to be taken just as it presented itself without a prejudice touching what it really must be. This seems like an excellent principle even though it was soon confined in practice to extensive and repetitive analyses of those old banalities of perception. Yet, can we not now bring into view another domain of objectivities, those which can only present themselves to the intuitive imagination, in a word, the "flora and fauna of surrealism." If those flora and fauna were usually examined in the light of aesthetics, as instituting a new style or fashion in the arts, perhaps if we take them with more seriousness, they can offer us some decisive insights into metaphysics. Surrealism itself always had to defend itself against any exclusively aesthetic direction; and does not the very contrast, real-surreal itself insist upon the inherently philosophical ambitions of the movement?

A cursory overview of the surrealist domain shows us melting watches, fur teacups, giraffes with their manes blazing, boots that terminate in feet, flatirons with tacks on the bottom, machines that cannot work, landscapes that on second glance are human faces, portraits that equally are bowls of flowers, or chateaux at the bottom of wells, as well as the limitless variety of beings that are constructed analogically and exist therefore only in poetic metaphor: "seasons luminous like the interior of an apple from which a slice has been cut out"; "This morning the daughter of the mountain is holding on her knees an accordion of white bats"; "the earth blue like an orange"; the "sun which shines at night"; and so on.

If we now take a step backward and generalize, perhaps a few structural features of this domain might appear. These beings are inherently constructed by metaphor, and therefore exist solely for the imagination. They are therefore inherently analogical and nonliteral. If a Dali stated his ambition to paint picture postcards of his dreams, or Magritte and Ernst to offer *precise* and *vivid* images, experiencing these as literal views of funny objects would be to miss the point; they are surrealist only by virtue of their strangeness, of their appeal to the imagination rather than to the literal eye. They are metaphorical syntheses of elements which might exist independently; but synthesized together, they can be only for the imagination. Breton finally declared that *everything* could be analogized with *everything* else, and with that universal analogy the distinctions which individuate and separate this from that fall away and with them the significance of literal discourse.

Chance and coincidence serve to form another class of beings. The surrealists were always looking for and cherishing strange coincidences, holding themselves open and ready for astrological predictions, fortune-telling, premonitory dreams, and the rest. The surrealist flora and fauna are frequently beings with contradictory properties, pure ephemera that exist only in an absolute instability. These beings obviously generate themselves spontaneously and have only coincidental consequences; they are births without navel cords, with no natural children. Alfred Jarry laid its foundation in *pataphysics*, the science of what occurs by chance, practised by both Arp and Duchamp.

They are rarely pretty. Most frequently they are obscene, offensive, horrid, and immoral; André Breton declared that no one exceeded him in bad taste. Some have seen in this only bravado or the desire to shock or a pathological streak of morbidity. But in a moment we shall look at precisely the function of the *moral* in defining that ontology of the real, which surrealism is opposing.

In addition to surrealist beings, there is also surrealist behavior. Some surrealists were given to sudden hysterical outbursts; hysteria was in fact much prized by Breton himself. Others passed an extraordinary amount of time in offensive public demonstrations and in simulating mental derangements: sleep-walking, disassociation, paranoia, automatism, Rimbaud's "systematic derangement of all the senses," black humor; and Péret was famous for his insults, crossing the streets of Paris to spit on priests, waiting in vain for them to turn the other cheek. For them the criminal, childish, insane, and primitive were cultivated as offering a new view out onto the possible.

Now our question returns: what has all this to do with

metaphysics? Metaphysics, or now phenomenological ontology, has more or less been the phenomenology of rather ordinary things, the so-called real world. And, for all the variations of analysis, that world remains composed of substances, identifiable and continuant, with regular properties, engaging in causal relations that fall under scientific or phenomenological law, or that exemplify universal concepts and together compose a real world. The picture to be sure is altered with Sartre's *pour-soi* and *en-soi;* with Heidegger's *Dasein, Zuhandensein* and *Vorhandensein,* but even with these reorientations the world that was thematic was the old real world. If existential ontologists distinguish between clock time and lived time, lived time itself for all its differences has its own peculiar structure, is susceptible to analysis, and behaves as a sort of a priori. It is most definitely not surrealist time. If lived space is not physical or geometric space, it still has its own a priori structures, near–far, up–down, oriented around my project; surrealist space is something altogether different, since surrealism changes the project. If the existentialists insist upon the foundational role of being-in-the-world, such that it is the source of all meanings, surrealism suggests that the world is foundational also for meanings that are surreal to that reality. Surrealist flora and fauna therefore bear one reference to the old real world and are never pure abstractions or nonobjectivities. But the other reference carries them elsewhere into a domain of the marvelous, the nonsubstantial but ephemeral, the evanescent, the contradictory present in Breton's conception of beauty as *explosante-fixe.* The surrealist interconnection is never the familiar causal one, nor the Heideggerian "for the sake of," binding together equipment for the projects of *Dasein.* The Heideggerian–pragmatic conception of beings as utilities for us has given way to the absolutely useless surrealist object. Everything here is coincidental. The flora and fauna do not exhibit universal categories; each is unique and, in its self-contradiction, not susceptible to conceptualization. If real things are those which are accessible to public observation, survey, or use, surreal things live solely in the domain of private imagination. If the entities of traditional or existential analysis compose finally a "world," those of surrealism do not; here everything is discontinuous, dislocated, disoriented, nonadditive, and so not a world at all.

There are, then, remarkable differences between the ontology of surrealism and that of either ordinary empiricism and its extension into science, or existential–phenomenological analyses. If there are ontological differences, there are also *moral* differences. The favorite entities of the surrealist domain are immoral, obscene, offensive, or disagreeable. Its humor is black, with a marked preference for the cruel, evil, disruptive, shocking. Favorite authors are the Marquis de Sade, Lautréaumont, Alfred Jarry, Jacques Vaché, all of whom are as unacceptable to civil society as the flora and fauna of surrealism are to our habitual sense of reality. Breton in one moment declared the perfect surrealist act to be that of discharging a revolver at random in a crowd, a remark which the highly conscientious Breton spent much time later qualifying. In any event, what lies behind this predilection for the black and satanic side of the moral world? If we look at it simply as itself evil and intolerable, we may get good grades for personal morality, but we should, I think, miss its deeper meaning, which after all was never simply to institute a new set of social or personal ethics in which cruelty would be tolerated.

We are here talking now of a *concrete* morality, the morality, choices, and preferences we live in, rather than of an abstract definition of the good or duty. And obviously we are all more or less decent people. We wish both to be and to have to be, on pain of exclusion from our own society. And so if there is for our realist ontology something like the real world, for our lived moral life there is a moral world held together by a mutual recognition of permissible or admirable behavior. And, if that moral world offers us a great and substantial good, at the same time it exacts a cost: a permanent blindness to what lies on the other side. And what lies on the other side is the radical freedom of Satan. In this mythology the question is whether the Fallen Angel did or did not see something hidden from Omniscience. The old surrealists always had a secret preference for the insights from the perspective of Satan; he alone was absolutely free, and surrealism is explicitly the cultivation of an absolute freedom. This freedom could be cultivated by experiencing the deliverances of subconscious desire, always obscene, or imaginatively committing atrocities (cold-blooded murders, acts of vampirism), promoting world catastrophes, committing suicide (of which there are an extraordinary number among the surrealists), delivering unprovoked insults, and so on. Once in *practice* they even went so far as to steal a waiter's pocketbook, but were immediately overcome with remorse and returned it. Now surely the meaning in all this is to free our moral sentiments from the ultimacy of the good and right. Without that freedom both right and wrong lose their significance and become merely the accepted, the bourgeois. The absolute delight in the perspective of evil, total liberation, and revolt was cultivated not so much for its thrills as for its value as a means of attaining that ultimate point of consciousness where contradictories cease to be perceived as opposites. And so ultimate liberation of the spirit required that it liberate itself profoundly from the ultimacy of the "moral." Something higher than the good was at stake, a daring of the absolutely ultimate. Nietzsche was not far away with his "beyond good and evil," nor Kierkegaard with his "teleological suspension of the ethical."

If surrealist ontology frees us from the horizon of the real, and surrealist ethics from that of the moral, these two aspects are surely not unrelated. It would not be difficult to demonstrate that for almost the entire history of metaphysics, the real and the good were derivative or convertible terms. Being and Value were the same, seen perhaps from different angles. For Plato, Being was the One; but that was the Good. For Aristotle, thought thinking thought was one conception of the highest being; it was also blessedness. For Christian theology, God was at one and the same time reality and holiness. The analogies in Spinoza and Leibniz and the major convictions of Western ontology through Hegel are not difficult to trace. In more recent or more empirical or "scientific" times, the pattern still holds. For the empirical temper what is real hovers around our practical *control* of things; the investigation of the *real* world in which we must willy-nilly live, at bottom, is within the horizon of the *useful,* just as both Heidegger and Dewey said. What we credit as real, therefore, bears a strict correlation with what we ultimately prize.

To whatever extent this is true, it is not surprising, then, that to take seriously the domain of the imagination, the surrealist domain, we must first radically change what we prize. Otherwise, what it offers presents itself as foolish, silly, irrelevant, useless, as indeed it all is judged from a morality bound to the useful, but as it is not, judged from its own perspective, absolute liberation.

Breton, pursuing absolute freedom along the route of beauty, accordingly had to redefine that old value. It was no longer the harmonious, the ordered, or the aesthetically pleasing; there is no beauty without the *marvelous,* and everything marvelous is beautiful, he said. And the marvelous? It was not the world of miracles, which Breton rejected, but what addressed that point of consciousness where opposites cease to be perceived as such. This in itself is already the supreme scandal to reason; but curiously enough it was the focus of another, more arcane tradition in philosophy, the philosophers of the "coincidentia oppositorum," the *Abgrund* and *Ungrund* of an Ekhardt, the mystical nature philosophies of Boehme and Novalis, and finally Hegel, whose Absolute Mind was precisely such a synthesis of opposites, the supremely living and supremely creative and supremely free. If Hegel was also the supremely rational dialectician, it was only after he had thoroughly revamped the very idea of Reason. And Hegel was one of the few traditional philosophers the surrealists admired. If the self-contradiction is anathema to the logical because everything can be deduced from it, it is for that very reason accepted by philosophers looking for the absolute principle of creativity and freedom; to them it appears not as a logical monstrosity, but as the most fecund principle of all.

In spite of the inveterate hatred of the surrealists for anything smacking of religion, one could easily find religious-minded philosophers probing in the same domain. For both Kierkegaard and Chestov, Reason could only envisage the necessary, essential connections, analytic implications, and since freedom cannot exercise itself in a domain of the necessary, the belief in the rationally absurd was itself essential to the life of freedom. Either logic or freedom must cede; this itself was a moral or existential choice, and each choice had its corresponding ontologies. Chestov puts the matter bluntly: for God, either all things are possible or not. And Chestov means "all things" literally, such as obliterating the past, affirming the contradictory. Only if all things are possible for God can the believer in God remain free. But a God for whom all things are possible is isomorphic with that point of consciousness which ceases to perceive the contradictory character of contradictories. Such a point of consciousness is infinite in the strictly Hegelian sense: if the finite is what is limited by its other, or opposite, the infinite is the synthetic union of something with what limits it; incorporating its own limit, it is positively infinite.

But if Hegel sometimes disappears into the abstract, for the surrealists all this was a matter of actual experience. It was not so much a matter of defining the point, as existing here and now within it. They are not, therefore, theoreticians so much as men pursuing that point guided by the surrealist sensibility, perhaps most purely that of Breton himself.

In any event, what I do believe emerges from a consideration of surrealism and philosophy is a point of more general interest, namely, that what we have always and shall continue to deem "real," the ancient and perpetual pursuit of philosophy, is itself a function of what each man radically chooses, that is, the face which value presents to him. Even in common discourse the "real" is seldom an indifferent matter of fact that can be ascertained by value-free procedures. It almost invariably connotes as well what is ultimately *important*. And with that connotation we have every right to inspect the notion of "importance" functioning, and every right in principle to bring it before our own freedom, for judgment. And conversely, if reality is made synonymous with mere fact, such that values are something else altogether, that distinction itself rests upon a prior option, which *is* an option or decision and not itself one more undismissable "fact."

Ontology from this light ceases to be a species of general science or the neutral reading of facts available to anyone, which reading must inherently claim an interpersonal validity such that one is true and another false. Ontologies are in the last analysis interpretations of Being, which of itself is open to an infinity of interpretations. Which one we dwell with is a function of what we ultimately prize or choose. Ordinary morality discloses the world of ordinary morality with its corresponding ontology; it was therefore necessary for the surrealists to wrench the spirit free of that morality if any credit was to be paid to the ontological domain of the surreal. Between these two particular ontologies, or particular moralities, I think there is no superior criterion; there are *only* free options. One of these options that particularly appeals to me as the perfect surrealist act is that of seeing the real world itself as the strangest and most marvelous surrealist formation.

# Nine

◇◇◇

# *Subjectivity and Philosophy*

THE PROBLEM "existentialism and metaphysics" might at first glance look like a question to which there might be some definite answer. A second glance discloses an insuperable dificulty: there are no definitive texts in either metaphysics or existentialism. Without further qualification, neither of the titles names anything more than an aspiration of thought; but as soon as that aspiration is fulfilled we no longer have metaphysics but rather the metaphysics of . . . an Aristotle, a Descartes, a Kant, a Hegel, or a Whitehead. And existentialism is in the same boat: *whose* existentialism? Is there a single philosopher associated by others with that movement who now accepts the title? Some wish to see in all of this some progress, each thinker correcting or improving his predecessors; but I know of no predecessor who accepts the improvement. Perhaps these titles should be regarded more as Kantian Ideas, never exhaustible but illustrable in an infinite variety. In any event, without the possibility of canonical texts for either metaphysics or existentialism, we might usefully extract for discussion a *theme* that can be illustrated by a number of existential and metaphysical works. Let that theme be the dialectical relation between subjective existence and its subjective thinker on the one hand, and the absolute being of its metaphysician on the other. What could these two aspirations have to say to each other?

If by "metaphysics" we understand the effort to define and grasp absolute being, that, in other words, which is in and perhaps for itself, that which is not a part, moment, or phase of anything else; and if by "existentialism" one understands the effort to think existence as it is subjectively for an existing man—then indeed there was a pronounced antipathy between the two from the start. In one paradigmatic case Kierkegaard looked upon Hegel's Absolute as impossible of realization. Who was to grasp it? An existing man could understand himself only after he no longer existed; and it is hard to imagine what help that could be. So long as there is subjective existence, then there is something unfinished and undecided. And so Hegel appears to Kierkegaard as a "comical" figure who forgot that he existed and, as alive, was *not* identical with God. But Hegel in anticipation was not without resources for a reply. If there are parts there must be a whole on pain of a mere part identifying itself with that whole. And so his entire effort was to comprehend how the parts presupposed the whole; subjectivity was indistinguishable from *error* in the domain of knowledge and from *criminality* in the domain of ethics. It is precisely *from* subjectivity that the philosopher must free himself. Hegel succeeded admirably in his own person; his answers to his critics suppressed the first-person pronoun and came out: "*Philosophy* can take no notice of your objection. . . ."

It would not be hard to multiply examples. For Nietzsche the metaphysical impulse was represented by Christianity with its God, eternal values, and otherworldliness. Nietzsche in revolt says: "*Against* the eternal, the value of the briefest, more perishable, the most seductive glints of gold on the belly of the Serpent, *Vita.*" Metaphysics in this light was nothing but an intellectual and vital degeneration.

The contemporary inheritors of existential thought continue in the same vein. For the Heidegger of *Sein und Zeit* Being is no longer absolute but is ultimately disclosed to existing man in resolute historical decision made in the light of death. For Sartre we can find nothing but *detotalized* totalities; man is wholly surrendered over to his world, must be wholly engaged "without transcendental escape-hatches," is in anguished and perpetual flight from where he is to where he can never arrive. Again, for both, the final point of view is that of existing man;

there can be no final survey since existence is always an unfinished project.

And yet, it is far from certain that these two apparently opposed directions of thought have not terminated the debate permaturely. If some existentialists insist upon the radical finitude of man's life and conclude to the impossibility or irrelevance of metaphysics, it may be they are right for *certain* metaphysics but not all; *or* that they have not examined human existence with the care it deserves. I believe they would be right against any metaphysics that conceived its absolute on the model of anything whatsoever objective, that is, "nature," "substance," "eternal form," "law," or "principle." I am urging not that there are no such things, but that they could not possibly illuminate lived subjective experience. Nor could any ontology that aspired to completeness omit subjectivity as an *irreducible* category. And if the term "Being" has a traditional connotation as what finally *is*, then the existentialists are right in insisting that either Being is so comprehensive as to mean nothing, or else, as naming *what is*, it is wholly inadequate to comprehend even the most elementary factors of subjective existence with its perpetual wrestling with what is not, with possible being, and with what ought to be. If Being aims at the essential and the necessary, again it renders itself irrelevant to subjective existence, where, if anything, "accidents" like birth and death become "essential" to its concerns, and where the necessary is precisely what can *not* be decided.

At the same time suppose that metaphysics is an expression of a deeper impulse of which such notions as absolute being are only figurative transcriptions? Perhaps metaphysics has been aiming at something final, but whose finality is ill conceived as a Being, like the famous sphere whose center was everywhere and circumference nowhere, variously used to describe the universe and God. If some forms of metaphysics look like pervasive category mistakes, is it not also clear, as Schopenhauer said, that man is a metaphysical animal, and that this aim at finality is *not* the historical product of certain mistakes made early in human thought? Perhaps, then, if we look again at human existence we might be able to see in its subjective form the roots of that very metaphysical aim which later translates itself into the effort to define "absolute being." This seems fair, since if metaphysics wishes to conclude too rapidly to absolute being, perhaps the existentialists have also concluded too rapidly to some essentially finite character of human existence; human existence, too, is inexhaustible and unsurveyable, as Jaspers insists; no one can give an exhaustive account of it, even when he is called an "existentialist." I should therefore like to tilt the discussion; instead of confining metaphysics to the pursuit of absolute being and ruling it out at once, perhaps if we chose a vaguer term, something like "finality," we might discover the subjective roots of such a pursuit, something deeper than logical blunders. And if instead of assuming we already know the very essence of human existence either as *Dasein* or *Pour-soi*, we leave that an open question and look into modes of existence *other* than that of being "surrendered over to the world in care," it is possible we may find embedded in subjective existence that very finality which otherwise looks dubious and problematical. For this project it would be promising to look at human existence in its provisional *successes* rather than its foundering and failure. And where can we begin to discover these successes? For me the least questionable formula would be that of André Breton, who defined surrealism as the celebration of *love, poetry,* and *liberty.* Following Breton no further than this formula, my own fondness for the phrase arises from the suggestion that perhaps in these very places we may find the roots of that impulse which made Schopenhauer see man as the "metaphysical animal"; at very least no one will be able to object that love, poetry, and liberty were invented by certain spurious reasonings of philosophers unacquainted with the blessings of modern logical analysis.

### Love

It certainly requires no argument to establish the decisive importance of love for human existence; if we had found out we were metaphysically condemned to anguish, no doubt we would have given up the whole business long ago as not worth the candle. Strange that its importance has to be argued for

metaphysics, which has preferred to discover reality everywhere else: in logic, mathematics, physics, astronomy, or in the
faculties of perception and reasoning insofar as they are
directed to that same physical or logical world. Perhaps the
neglect of love by metaphysics could be traced to an initial
error that regards love as an "emotion," properly to be treated
by psychology, rather than a mode of *being* of central
importance to metaphysics. That mode of being, for all of its
enigmas, can be sketched out simply for our present purposes:
two are in love when each finds the other essential to his or her
existence. Together they constitute a whole, in fact, an
*absolute* whole, complete in itself. Aristophanes' tale in the
*Symposium* is instructive on the matter and says all that need
be said: in the *beginning* there were only *complete* beings, so
self-sufficient that even the gods were jealous of their independence and pride: so each was split; and historical existence
is but the history of each half pursuing his other half. In love
that other half is found and there is a temporary and
provisional restoration of the primordial whole. And, no doubt,
some such thing is what every lover would say: in the embrace
there is that finality in which there can be no other or higher
values, in which nothing external is needed or wanted; a
finality within experience and time for which the rest of
human existence is only a nostalgia. The poetry of love, where
all this finds direct expression, dilates endlessly on the theme:
lovers regard each other as "gods" and "goddesses"; in love
they are in "heaven"; their love is "eternal"; it is the "meaning
of life," and so forth. From age to age and culture to culture
the language is the same; it comes so close to religious
enthusiasm and exaltation that churches begin to find it
blasphemous. And the categories lovers spontaneously use are
so outrageous to a metaphysics or epistemology based on the
natural sciences or mere sense perception that they must be
immediately explained away: reason has been clouded by
passion. Even common sense has its own refutations: how
could their love be eternal when they hadn't met the day
before yesterday and perhaps their eyes are wandering before
they even finished their poetic phrases? How can they be in
heaven, when as anyone can see they have just checked into

the motel? How can they "know" each other, in the curiously ambiguous Elizabethan phrase, when they have only constructed each other out of sense data aided by logical connectors and, moreover, are notoriously subject to delusions? How can any such thing be the "meaning of life" when there are other pressing matters to attend to such as making a living, cooking, and politics? The truth would be that love is not so much subjective existence discovering absolute finality, as an illness, something like an "epileptic fit," as Susan Sontag recently put it.

And yet, what do these criticisms amount to but misunderstandings basing themselves upon a metaphysics of the third person, observing certain objective phenomena and interpreting them under principles adequate only for objective phenomena seen third-personally? But the phenomenology of human existence must begin (and for me also *end*) with that existence *as it is to those living it;* for anyone to examine his own existence as if it were that of *another* is to introduce schizophrenia into the very heart of philosophic method. If we are condemned to regard things external to us impersonally and as objects, there is one form of being, happily, which is not external to us nor an object; that, of course, is ourselves. With the critical acceptance of the testimony of lovers, we may have the beginning of the solution to our initial question concerning the subjective roots of metaphysical meanings; the human mind would never in the first place have embarked on an effort to define and grasp something called the Absolute if it had not encountered a *form* of it in its own direct experience. In love, according to the testimony of the world's lovers, human existence finds finality "for a moment" in *value*, in *knowledge*, and in *being*. This finality, I should emphasize, is *found* and is not a theory, hypothesis, or construct.

### Poetry

If metaphysics has traditionally preferred to think about the whole universe to thinking about love, whenever it seeks to base itself on language and the a priori conditions for intelligible discourse, it habitually turns to the literal prose of daily scientific or logical discourse, and it shows a marked tendency to avoid poetry, which not by accident is the spontaneous language of lovers. If love has been taken to be an emotion rather than a mode of being, poetry equivalently has been taken to be noncognitive "emotive expression," containing neither information nor analysis, neither true nor false but at best pleasing or displeasing: in effect it is, so considered, but a prolonged sigh or groan. Of if this seems too crude for belief, certain poetry may be admitted under the title of "rhymed science," didactic verse such as that of Lucretius and the many rhymed versions of Darwin's evolution in the nineteenth century. Here the "poetic" element resides in the external forms of rhythm, rhyme, and elevated diction. No wonder poetry is lightly taken by metaphysics; it is nothing but a metaphorical, hence confusing, way of saying what could be more clearly said in literal prose.

But this notion of poetry would be spurned by authentic poets as the very definition of bad poetry. Literal, scientific propositions, and those of metaphysics insofar as it apes the sciences, are propositions that are true or false about a subject matter *which can be encountered independently of the proposition in question;* in short, they are true or false about a world which is as it is independently of what the proposition or system of propositions says of it. When a sentence says of something how it is, and it is that way, then the sentence is "true." On the other hand a poem is *about* nothing whatsoever which is or can be given *independently of that poem.* The play *Hamlet* is not and was never intended to be true or false about the historical Prince of Denmark. If it is about anything, it is about the Hamlet who is given to us in the play itself and *there alone.* And so with all poetry; Blake's "Tiger" is hardly a contribution to zoology. And yet poetry is a *disclosure,* a disclosure of what is available to us only through it. Since its content is accessible only through the poem itself, the disclosure is not subject to correction, confirmation, or disconfirmation through independent observation, experiment, science, or history in general. In *Hamlet* I do indeed *see* something, persons in action and passion; *Hamlet* is, then, a disclosure and not a mode of blindness; but what is disclosed is accessible to us only through the poem itself. A disclosure *of any form whatsoever* falls under the general category *truth*, and so it is not surprising that poems are also judged as "true" and "false"; but these terms must be understood as equivalent to the poem's own internal power and coherence of disclosure, that is, to the completeness of disclosure, rather than as true to some independent reality. In this sense when the terms "true" and "false" are used of poetry in general, including novels, they must be taken as synonyms for completeness and coherence of disclosure, a criterion internal to the poem and identical with the purely poetic value of the poem. Thus "false" poems are bad poems in purely poetic terms: a false Hamlet would be a Hamlet radically incoherent with himself or shown acting without intelligible motivation or with the relevant situation and consequences of his action incompletely given.

With the introduction of terms such as "coherence" and "completeness" as synonyms for truth and falsity within a poem, not much would need to be said to bring our discussion well within the sphere of the idealist conception of truth as systematic coherence. "Truth is the Whole," Hegel said; and, so conceived, there is no separate, independent whole *of* which it is true. And so the Hegelian system itself might be conceived as a vast poetic whole to be measured only by its comprehensiveness and coherence; similarly, each poem taken by itself exhibits the same characteristics: each discloses for us a whole, the whole of that poem. As wholes, they are *in principle* forbidden from being additive in their disclosures. King Lear, Macbeth, and Hamlet could not have roles in a "larger play"; we are not invited to wonder what they were doing before they are disclosed to us; nor what their friends do after the final curtain is rung down. If, then, in *scientific* discourse we are introduced into a domain of speech and thought where each new proposition adds to our total knowledge of its subject, a domain that is endless, in poetry we experience a world, a final whole that needs completion or addition only to the extent that the poem *fails* in the disclosure of its own theme. And, finally, since we ourselves, as *animalia metaphysica*, have a nostalgia for something final and absolute, when we experience imaginatively and poetically what we have been looking for, we have a perfectly understandable joy; each poem in effect is a celebration of its own accomplishment, the disclosure of an absolute within human experience. Even tragedies, of course, are fundamentally celebrations *not* of the deaths of their heroes but of that final whole which for the Greeks was divine Fate, but which for *us* most often is the act of poetry itself in the creator as well as his audience, which now is renewed. Poetry, then, taken as including all the arts, is an experienced celebration of the disclosure of something final and absolute within existence itself.

## *Liberty*

Both love and poetry are expressions of human freedom; if we were not free *not* to love, what would our love be worth? And if, as poets, we could not liberate ourselves from our own instinctive sympathies and antipathies for our characters, how could we perceive that finality within which they *all* have their essential justification? Both lovers and poets, then, *enact* what might *otherwise* look like only a conjectural condition of man: liberty. But liberty is enacted also in decision. Let us recall some basic factors in decision as they appear to one deciding, if not from the standpoint of an external observer, let alone a metaphysician already provided with a total "theory of being." I cannot decide anything unless, of course, it appears to me that there is something to be determined by that decision; there must be alternatives now open that my decision will close. Further, *I* must make up my mind; that is, my decision decides what stand I shall take toward open alternatives. If my mind is already made up, then indeed I am not *then* deciding but *already* decided. And what is it I decide? For action, for what I shall do. And so my own action must appear to me open to my own disposition or I cannot appear to myself to be deciding anything. Finally, it must appear *up to me*, up to me and *no one* or *nothing* else. If it is up to me, then I must appear free to decide to myself. The freedom in question is a freedom from compulsion from anything *not-me*. But what counts as me and what as not-me? In the present context I would count as not-me anything I had *not* chosen or consented to; the question, then, is *not* some *factual* question as to the *actual* composition of me, which would lead into problems as to whether my body, my id, my inclinations, my desires are or are not to be reckoned as "parts" of me; the *question* is decided in this context *by myself:* if I *consent* to these determinants, *affirm* them, or if I decide according to a "moral principle," then any of these factors, since they are determinant of me *only* through *my* approval or consent, must be reckoned as being "part of me"; in short, in the present context what *is* me and what is *not* is itself decided by my own free decision and is *not* an independent, scientific, or psychological question. Thus, a man who *consents* to slake his thirst is not aware that he is being *compelled* by an external force, thirst; he has made the thirst *his* by his *consent* to it. Vice versa, if he *resisted,* then the thirst *would* appear as "external" to him; but his resistance would at the same time demonstrate that he was free from its compulsion over him. If he resisted but succumbed anyway, either he was *not* free from his thirst, in which case it would no longer be called a decision but rather a compulsion, or he would have prima facie evidence that his resistance was in bad faith.

Decision, then, is one primordial locale of experienced freedom. Freedom, as Kant demonstrated, is nothing that can be illustrated in external experience or even in internal experience if that is understood as composed of "inner *feelings*"; freedom is not a feeling at all but, again, a mode of *subjective being;* being independent of external compulsion. There are feelings accompanying free decision, of course, but they can range everywhere from Sartrean anguish to the delirium and exaltation of a Nietzsche. The free man is in an ontological solitude, an origin without support; and that mode of being can be either dreaded or welcomed. But in either case we come back to our chief concern here: the mode of being that is freedom is itself formally identical with our old friend the Absolute. The Absolute also is in ontological solitude depending upon nothing else, since everything else is but a part or phase of it. In short, existing men in their subjective liberty are like so many gods; Descartes showed that our own freedom was infinite and therefore equal to that of God, although our understanding lagged far behind.

All of which may seem a somewhat romantic exaltation of commonplace occurrences. Is it really necessary to invoke something absolute to account for every daily decision? I do believe indeed that it is; but perhaps this contention can be made more plausible by considering decisions that are terminal. If our daily decisions hardly decide more than how prechosen goals might best be reached, let us call terminal those decisions in which I decide where I take my stand toward *my own existence as such*, that is, what I will die for. Here my freedom reaches its apogee; what I decide in favor of must appear to me as a "final value," that which *must* unconditionally be. The unconditionality of such values can include the whole world, as in the old motto: "Let justice prevail or let the world be destroyed." Or with Socrates, Luther, and Bruno we see examples of decisions that placed a final value on the question of the decider's very existence. Our own question does not concern the wisdom of their decisions or any further analysis of exactly what it was that each felt he was deciding. All we need is the phenomenology of the terminal decision: to each something of final value was decided, the alternative to which appeared to him incompatible with the value of his own existence. And further, what was decided was in the domain of *contingent existence*. It would be foolish for a man to sacrifice his life to prove that there was or was not another planet in the solar system or to prove Gödel's theorem. These matters are as they are and no man's sacrifice can alter the evidence; on the other hand it may be decisive whether such problems can be *discussed* in society or whether political authority has any proper jurisdiction over them. And so the final decision decides subjective existence, seen now as having alternatives, one of which is finally to be rejected. In the unconditionality of such decisions a free man attaches himself finally to something absolute; in such decisions is it not apparent that metaphysics, aiming at the absolute, finds its subjective roots?

# Ten

◇◇◇

# *Philosophy as Autobiography*

THE ORIGINS of philosophy are obscure, and the obscurity is such that it cannot be dispelled by further historical information. Any account whatsoever of the origins of philosophy is strictly dependent upon the philosophy of him who gives the account, and eventually it will be that philosophy whose origin is given. We thus enter into a circle where the relevant facts are determined by our principles, in fact those very principles which are to be accounted for or justified by the facts. Heidegger dubs it a hermeneutical circle; Hegel also sees it as the circle of a system. But if circles are causes of despair in deductive logic, circular reasoning being the same as no reasoning at all, for philosophy the situation is not the same. At least perhaps we can agree that not all circles are equally valuable: they can differ in *range* and in *coherence*. As for range, perhaps the smallest circle imaginable is that of Parmenides, for whom the truth is confined to the perception that *being is one*. Plato's dialogue *Parmenides* even questioned whether this much could be said with perfect coherence. In any event, the diameter of Parmenides' circle is very small indeed, every statement of change, difference, time, and multiplicity being excluded from the circle of the truth. The coherence within the circle is *almost* perfect; the *unity of being* is on the verge of perfect identity between "being" and "unity"; when they exactly coincide into exact unity of meaning, then the circle becomes a point, and we achieve perfect coherence within a zero range, a somewhat short-winded termination of the project.

I know of no circle larger than Hegel's nor at the same time one more contested for its coherence. My present purpose is not to defend Hegel but to look once again at the obscure origins of philosophy, betraying thereby my own philosophical predilections, and in the end to offer reasons to justify the occupation of a particular standpoint, the autobiographical. In the end this project too will be circular and not demonstrative. That is, the reasons will be autobiographical choices for considering philosophy itself as a gigantic autobiographical confession in depth. *Being is autobiographical.*

To return to our theme: the origins of Western philosophy in Greece have been told many times. In the beginning there seemed to be a single human type: it is questionable whether he was what we would call a Philosopher, Scientist, Priest, or Poet. Or, if one can force these roles together, perhaps he was a Sage. But it is indeed *for us* a conglomeration of functions, which we now think we have happily and clearly distinguished. Religion is an affair of ritual and "faith"; the arts offer us "aesthetic pleasures"; philosophy is yet another department of the university where people "analyze" what others have said in order to make it clear. Truth is the possession of scientists who, even if they don't have it, nevertheless can define the methods by which it might be reached in an unforeseeable future. And so, if what is now called philosophy had its origins in Greek religion, it was a religion itself unlike anything of that name today; the arts too took their origin in religion, and yet, since the religion in question was already what we call "artistic" ritual or drama, what has been said? Or did religion take *its* rise from philosophy and the dramas of art? To be an origin is already to be obscure, since it can only be understood through precisely what those origins are taken to be the origin of. And then there is always the optical illusion of understanding things *as* origins; is it not doubtful indeed whether these prehistorical origins *took themselves* to be origins of something else altogether, finally ourselves, creatures they may very well have found hopelessly confused and fractured in spirit if they could have anticipated us? Perhaps we are exactly those fragments against which they held themselves together, to which they were most deeply opposed?

If we now trace a mythical or dialectical origin of philosophy, it will be retrospective story and will not necessarily correspond to temporal sequences. It will be an interpretation, in effect. And in that light the origins of what later degenerated into philosophy is the insight that *one equaled one*. Parmenides' "being is one" would serve equally well, but I can derive all I need from the simpler example, and we have authority from Plato himself; his Academy forbade anyone ignorant of mathematics from entering. Mathematics today is too complicated for anyone to understand as a whole; but we need only *one is one*. Most of us today are far too blasé to find anything of interest in that simple insight, but by the same token perhaps we have lost the extraordinary origins of that "rational thought" which philosophy aspires to be.

There are some horrible puzzles involved even in this simple equation: how can one equal itself, thereby becoming in a way *two*, when we had only one to begin with? A two, moreover, which are then seen to be not two but one? And what is one-half? We divide one into two, but how can a pure one be divided at all, when by definition it is not two of anything but only one? Everything becomes easy when we think not of a pure one but of *one thing*, and anyone can see that things can be divided into parts; but we began with pure numbers, not quantities of things in space or time, and with that fatal step pure numbers raise frightful problems. Impure numbers, numbers of things are easier, but then they are impure. In any event our problem now is not to explore precisely these problems which exercised the best minds of Greece but to reflect upon another matter: the origin of rational philosophy from thinking about numbers, in a sense in which *all* philosophy is *rational*, even when it is also empirical. Empirical philosophies are also rational in our present sense, since they still offer us a rational theory of experience and its contingencies and not an empirical theory of experience. What, then, is so striking about *one equals one* that some such insight is the origin of philosophy itself, where even the mind holding it as a model of truth or being is already a decomposition of the original unity, endeavoring to grasp reality itself in its deepest depths by means of the rational concept? Let us explore for a bit the excitement generated by the idea that one is one, and its by-products, the *concept* or *definition:* Socrates was held by Aristotle to be the inventor of the definition, and with that, rational philosophy. In Plato's version Socrates cautions us again and again only to follow the argument. Nay, he says frequently, you are disagreeing not with Socrates but with the argument, *Logos.* By following the argument, one's mind will be enabled to think what is, that is, Being. By losing track of the argument, the mind wanders, and it can hit the mark only by chance opinion; the arts of *rhetoric* then take over, emotional persuasion overwhelms clear insight, and one soon finds oneself in the hands of the sophists, who could make the better look like the worse, vice seem to be a virtue, with the consequence that both mind and heart became victims of the existent chance forces in all their ambiguity. Socrates, on the other hand, armed with little more than the tautology that it is always better to do good, was able to withstand the political forces of his fellow Athenians, remain true to his principles, and resist corruption unto death. A very noble story indeed, which has haunted philosophers ever since, supplying a justification for their pride in their pursuit and a confidence in its absolute value. Philosophy, then, is concerned with very serious matters: truth and error, virtue and vice, acceptable conditions of life and death; and it must work insofar as it remains faithful to its origins solely by reason, argument and tautology. It may seem that we are now far from *one equals one;* but are we when we recall that for the final reaches of Plato's philosophy the Good itself was seen to be The One?

More specifically, the pursuit of definitions, of clear concepts, of arguments that are deductive and therefore analytic are all so many forms of realizing the project of rational philosophy to know and know in the form of a variety of necessarily unified identities, each itself another version of the primordial unity, the one is one, with which the whole thing began. The power of the idea of unity is therefore enormous, and when Being itself is envisaged as the One, as with Parmenides and Plato, philosophy takes under its supervision the whole of reality *insofar as it may be understood in this way,* but that is the only way so far as rational philosophy is concerned.

Now that there is no inherent justification for this movement of thought is evident to me. Transcendentally considered, it is an *option,* which is neither more nor less justified than any other option. Once made, it defines a series of correlative terms—Being, Reason, Truth—and within it, alternatives must necessarily appear as mere Becoming, mere history, mere fact, mere opinion, or mere confusion, to sum it up. Now the confusion can be allayed, but only insofar as it is reducible back to essence, concept, definition, and eventually The One. Now this represents a very noble tradition indeed, and it is certainly not my purpose to scoff at it. But it is, I believe, of philosophical importance to define its limits, to look at it as one of an indefinite number of spiritual alternatives open to the mind, finally a *choice.* And if that choice is not made in the light of its alternatives, then indeed it is blind, and in an existential sense of the term no choice at all. Hence the purpose of what follows is to outline a fundamental alternative, philosophy as autobiographical, not for the purpose of compelling assent, but simply for the purpose of clarifying alternatives; with alternatives clarified, one's own transcendental freedom is given room to make an existential choice; but that choice itself will be of an *autobiographical* and not rational character since reason itself is at stake. Hence the interpretation of philosophy as autobiographical is itself yet another autobiographical choice. Thus, what is denied is that there is any compelling *reason* for any fundamental choice, thereby preserving one's freedom to the very end. The choice in question is how thought and reality are to be related.

What, then, is autobiography, why is it of any philosophical importance, and why does it hate "one is one"? Let me substitute the phrase, "autobiographical consciousness" for autobiography, since nothing here initially is at stake upon the *writing* of one's life. What is at stake is philosophy as a mode of consciousness, what it might be conscious of, and how it might inhabit a certain standpoint, the first-person singular.

If rational thought aims at the one, the concept, and implicit in that, the necessary, timeless truth of universal scope aiming at "objectivity," one need only note here what is *omitted* or reduced to a derived and secondary place, of course the exact opposite: the subjective in its subjectivity, the manifold, the unnecessary or accidental, the nonuniversal or the singular, the irreplaceable, unique, and historical. Not of course that these are ignored, but they have rational value only insofar as they exemplify grander rational principles or laws. In this vein Whitehead characterized metaphysics as a search for that set of irreducible principles which everything must exemplify. Let us for the sake of the argument agree that some such principles could be found; the next question concerns their cognitive *value* and what they *omit* or conceive of solely in terms of an illustrative value. And it is obvious at a glance that what is omitted is life itself as it is to those living it, *unless* they happen to be metaphysicians of this stamp. Hence, while for rational philosophy it is a decisive refutation to tell a man that his arguments are *only* of autobiographical interest, that is to say, of no interest whatsoever to philosophy, it would be either ludicrous or insane for a man to tell himself that his own life were of *merely* autobiographical interest to *him*; what else might there be?

It is, then, this sense of the ontological preciousness of existence in its unrepeatability and singularity that animates the autobiographical consciousness. To live a life in order to exemplify principles that one cannot help but exemplify and that could just as easily be exemplified by anyone else and in fact must be so exemplified, and not merely any*one* else but absolutely everything which is, is tantamount to declaring one's *own* life meaningless and insignificant in its greatest depth. And the same goes when one's aim is somewhat *less* than the absolutely metaphysical of absolutely unrestricted generality; is there some particular obligation for any existing man to live his life in order to know the specific laws of human nature, supposedly common to all? If there is some such nature, which we all willy-nilly exemplify, then it can well take care of itself and certainly has no need of anyone's individual support. Further, if the very conception of a universal *human nature* can only look upon human history as variations upon a known theme, if our metaphysics finally agrees to look at history as the scene where our lives are played out, we have made *some* progress, but hardly enough. We have at least perceived that history is a unique record of what men have made of themselves, and this required a making in which universal concepts and unities were more or less beside the point. For while concepts like "human history," "*the* historical event," "laws of history," Heidegger's "historicity," etc. may be true enough, they serve only to omit from history that which is historical and to transform it once again into an illustration of supposedly knowable generalities. History itself is then required to feed its data into a general theory of man or even an "objective record," supposedly the desired issue of a study of history. And obviously all this from ground up is a far cry from history as it is historically lived.

I believe, then, that we must go *all the way* in this direction, still pursuing an ultimate reality and an ultimate value, which perhaps are the same. We must, in other words, revert to the first-person singular consciousness of life, the autobiographical, in order to arrive at the foundations of an alternative to rational, objective philosophy. And curiously, we can accept help from one of the great rationalists, Descartes, with some essential modifications. The Cartesian *cogito ergo sum* was given as a central point beyond which one cannot go, an anchor so to speak in a world of external nature, of opinion, of the dubitable, but then it was exploited only for the indubitability of its clear and distinct ideas, for the sake of a rational reconstruction of the world. The rational and, in Descartes' case, mathematical reconstruction of the world is one project; the nonrational, lived recuperation of life is another, which we are looking at here; but the original standpoint from which these projects project themselves is identical: I, the first-person singular, rooted in itself and nothing beyond, the origin of choices and decisions, as well as cognition. I as I am for myself.

Descartes' preoccupation, of course, was a mathematical physics that was in principle certain and indubitable and from which he expected and got an unforeseeable wealth of practical results. Now we have but to turn the same *cogito, I think,* elsewhere, back to its own unrepeatable existence to disclose another domain. From this domain I believe NO practical benefits will result, no contributions to psychology, to sociology, to political theory, to the theory of human nature; nothing of this order for whatever it is worth is our present concern. What is our concern, pursuing the autobiographical consciousness, is the recuperation in mind of the very life of the man living it. This too has its clarity, although that clarity is in principle different from what Descartes or Spinoza sought. The rational clarity of clear and distinct ideas, or with Spinoza "adequate ideas," must be limited to those things of which an adequate idea *can* be formed. And yet, while this does define one order of clarity, referred to above as conceptual, definitional, and reducible eventually to the "one is one," it is hardly the only form. Life as we live it hardly has to wait for a clear and distinct idea to be formed of it in order to exhibit its own sense, meaning, or "clarity." Here, for a moment, the phenomenologists and ordinary language philosophers can join hands; the phenomenologists uncover the implicit *sense* of both experience and the experienced, which we daily enact and which, explicated with sufficient nuance, lends itself to fair articulation. We come out with accounts a good deal different from those of the rationalists, which nonetheless have their own clarity. Thus, if for Spinoza "love" is "pleasure accompanied by the representation of its cause," the phenomenologists such as Binswanger and others look at the intention that structures the passion, what the passion in and of itself aims at, its built-in intentionality; and while obviously in this new vein one can hardly expect a new formula so neat and absurd as Spinoza's, one is at least back in the human scene, where to love is to wish to *be* with another in a decisive mode. At this point the poets come into their own.

And so two things have happened: the very ego that lives emerges for itself as the unshakable center of its own life, but then the ego turns its attention not to the eternal and timeless, but to its own unique existence here and now in order to see what it is and how it is. The ego becomes reflexive on its own life. And it is important to note that the first-person singular standpoint, where the ego or self, sitting firmly upon itself, passes all in review before itself, is not in the least *narcissistic*.

It may well become so, as one of its transcendental possibilities, but that is its business. If it indeed recovers its own life as its essential theme, there is no reason in the world why it is compelled to think *about itself*. If it endeavors to recuperate its life, its life will of course not be a meditation upon itself *divested* of others or of the inter-subjective and objective world in which it lives. An ego so directed upon itself would very soon come to the end of its tether; there is nothing there. And yet that "nothing" makes all the difference in the world. Unless an *ego* lives a life, there is none lived; and if its life consists in nothing but a meditation upon itself divested of life, there is also no life. And so two things: the ego is indeed transcendental to any portion of its own life; and yet that transcendental self also lives.

The autobiographical consciousness, then, is at one and the same time transcendental and existential; it is in effect the consciousness of the transitory life of the transcendental ego. Phenomenology can take us so far; but then, armed now with existentialism, it seeks to turn life itself into yet another knowable structure. That is, it prefers philosophically to see in human existence those ever recurrent, ever depressing structures or essences which perpetually remain true and are perpetually irrelevant to the actual existent man living his own unique life. At that point existential thought, as in Heidegger and Sartre, betrays its own best insight. I believe Jaspers almost alone has remained faithful to the real situation, with his resolute refusal to present a new doctrine of what it is to live, what *Existenz* is and how it must understand itself. In any event, if existential thought *touches* upon the central subject, the ontological importance of life for him living it, it runs the radical risk of ruining everything by turning it too into a philosophical theme, with claimed structures, necessities, a priori essences, and the rest.

And so while existential philosophy comes close, it also comes closest to ruining everything. It retains the old nostalgia for an ever abiding truth, the universal, the "one is one," now applied to *life itself.*

And so what remains? Only what from the rational point of view looks like chaos, incommunicability, the absolutely trivial, in effect, the very domain from which it fled in the first place, life. I repeat that this itself is an autobiographical *choice*, with no transcendental reason against it, nor for it, but only built-in consequences or destinies.

If so much is to be said against life and its autobiographical understanding, what might for a change be said for it? What does life indeed offer? But at this precise point it must be obvious that *nothing* can be said in general except by way of negations. Dilthey said: "one cannot get behind life." And so, if we have already characterized the ontological domain of life in terms such as "unique," "irreplaceable," "singular," "accidental," this characterization, itself a general one, uses terms that are the mere negatives of rationally comprehensible ones. Reason can only understand essence, the "one is one," and while it can recognize that something lies beyond, it is sheer confusion to suppose that it can absorb or reduce what eternally lies beyond it to what is within its competence. And what lies beyond reason is only accessible to us because we are not ourselves exclusively reason, but existent conscious persons consciously living in a domain that is a scandal to our own reason.

That consciousness called here "autobiographical consciousness" is not in the least plunged into darkness, not in the least incommunicable or unintelligible. It stutters only when it tries to respond to questions posed to it by reason, such as "what is life," and respond, moreover, in rational terms. Left to itself, it is perfectly articulate. To imagine that Bertrand Russell alone possessed clarity and communicability, whereas Proust's *Remembrance of Things Past* is unintelligible, shows us nothing with its own clarity, and is a closed book to us would be, to put it mildly, an odd position. Or to think that Proust was intelligible only through the use of common nouns and universal predicates, that he made a contribution to the science of human nature, or that he badly needs clarification through some further analyses of logic, epistemology, psychology, or sociology would verge on the ludicrous. *Remembrance of Things Past* is fictional autobiography and presents itself as the attempt of M to recover past time. Not any past time, but M's past, his own unique singular past, and to raise that effort to consciousness. The consciousness of one man's past life is, of course, not in the form of deduction, analysis, or for the sake of an exemplification of general principles. It is *narrative*. As a narrative, it has no universal consequence. We are not all M's, we did not all live that life, see or do those things, nor could anyone else have done them. If the whole indeed is taken as of universal application, such that we must all say that *in the last analysis* we are all M's, that "last analysis" only signals once again our inherent propensity to abstract and generalize. In the last analysis I am M only in my capacity as being a human being, living at some time or other; but if that is all that is gotten from *Remembrance of Things Past*, we have indeed left the novel far behind and really have our attention on something else, a college-outline synopsis, far easier to write than the novel, far easier to commit to memory, and if the truth be told, far more profoundly wrong than right. Nothing whatsoever can be generalized from the novel without leaving the novel to that extent behind. Indeed what *need* has the novel of such modes of understanding? It is as intelligible as it can be in its own terms, gains nothing but impoverishment from generalization, and certainly offers itself not as an illustration of something already known to us but as a unique narration of singular events.

Let us suppose for the argument that some such thing were actually in fact the life of somebody, Marcel Proust in fact, a life which, while we know perfectly well was not his life, could have been. We should now have not fictional autobiography but real autobiography, the exploration and confession in depth of what one life meant to the man living it. This I should hold to be of absolute ontological value to us, as well as to him, *precisely in its irreplaceability*, its singularity. For if ontology or metaphysics is genuinely interested in what there is, why on earth should it direct any particular attention to universal Being, its first specification, cosmic nature, or finally even to Mind as such; granting that the acts and works of mind presuppose nature, they do not repeat it, but raise it to something generically distinct. And yet to go only so far is to miss the final, most determinate, most concrete, and ontologically richest domain of all: each precise singular life as lived by the man living it. And, finally not even that *as seen by another*, but as he himself achieves consciousness of it. This is the sole domain in which we have the possibility of *direct* access, to know from firsthand acquaintance what we are talking about, in effect, *to know ourselves.* And if someone should protest that one's own life is exactly that about which one knows least and is most subject to delusion, I think the reply must be either that we have shifted the sense of knowing *away* from subjective acquaintance *to* an objective, psychological, or sociological sense, *or* that the possibilities of self-delusion are themselves internal to that man's sense of life, and therefore a revealing part of it. If delusion is an internal thread in a man's life, then indeed it would falsify that life to try to do away with it. It should be confessed. If it is not internal, then it *is* a delusion only from the standpoint of some theory, psychoanalytic or other, which is holding that life up to criteria it may well itself have rejected.

And now a final extension of the point of view I have been exploring. Abstractly considered, a life is the life of a transcendental ego; it expresses its choices, its projects, its way of handling what its own life brings before it. That ego itself freely and absolutely *determines what shall have importance for it*. In fact, it is hardly different from that choice, and only in rare states would it ever deliberate the question; it *is* its choice, has the possibility of revoking or changing that choice, but nevertheless for any coherent stretch of life lives out its own choice of significance. It retrospectively *recovers* what its implicit choice was by narratively recovering to itself what it itself became.

Now, hidden in Proust were two absolute passions: his infinite preoccupation with the persons in his circle, and his equally infinite preoccupation with art, with salvation, in a word, a salvation deeply Platonic in character. Involuntary memory, linking together by immediate recognition two moments separated in time but linked together in essence and expressible in art, was his salvation from oblivion. Not all passed away forever, but the individual could recapture directly what had been long forgotten and was no longer accessible to willed recollection. And this gave him an intimation of the power of the work of art itself to save something from oblivion. My present point is not so much to explore these theories, but to consider at the end the role of philosophy itself, whether Proust's *or any other*, in existence. In Proust's life a tincture of philosophy is clearly inherent, which forms an essential part of his novel. And yet the novel remains a novel and not a literal philosophical demonstration. Putting philosophical reflections in a novel of the fictional autobiographical sort suggests a view which, while hardly Proust's, is nevertheless tenable; it brings us to our conclusion: philosophy as autobiography.

And with this formula I would like to offer a summary of what I have been arguing piecemeal above. At bottom, there is nothing but each of our human lives. But those lives have a transcendental pole, the I, whose life it is. The transcendental ego then must choose, that is, animate its existence with a meaning for itself, even if that meaning is the joy of meaninglessness. And, if it so chooses, it may try to tell the tale of its own life to itself and others. It will call that effort philosophy perhaps, if the word "philosophy" looms with any authority and if it deliberately rationalizes itself, subsumes itself under "one is one," or it may call it religion or art if those terms possess the required resonance. But, indeed, if the ego should be serious, it will try to express to itself the very deepest and closest sense it has of its life. If "metaphysics," "philosophy," "art," or perhaps even "politics" expresses what lies closest to the very choice of living that the self is, then its occupations will be directed accordingly, and its thought will be the thought inherent in those occupations.

In all of this I have been trying to reflect upon that peculiar preoccupation called philosophy, which aims at the highest and alas frequently sinks to the lowest. It is at its nadir when it is not an intuitive clarification of anyone's deepest interest, but a rationalistic, argumentative obfuscation of what is already evident. Philosophy properly taken is the articulation in thought of one man's deepest concerns. Those concerns traditionally are named reality, truth, and the good, meaning of course that few persons seriously wish to become unreal, fraudulent, spurious beings themselves. Or, if they do, they wish to do so voluntarily and with a certain relish. Or, no matter how much one may wish to fool others, and for a time even oneself, it would be a rare life indeed that wished most dearly to live itself out in self-delusion. Those would make fascinating autobiographies—but truth has that value, even if only as an ideal. As for the good, it becomes confused with reality, but, as the Greeks thought, for a man to pursue evil knowingly would be as ludicrous as for him to choose to be ill. If these ancient terms have lost all their power, perhaps what they express can be reanimated by a reversal of certain strains of rational thought, always looking for the general, the abstractly thinkable, the demonstrable. A reversal toward the first-personal life of the transcendental ego, reoccupying its own position, and finding within itself the possibility of an indefinite range of choices, which it nevertheless existentially refuses to make. The history of philosophy is the history, then, of the most profound choices men have made. If they *talk* as if a single, literal truth were at stake, were statable, that some approached it and others receded from it, or that there is a single line of general progress, it may be possible to understand these naive claims with some charity. Autobiographically understood, we see no more progress or development than we see among the various souls of whom these are the deepest confessions. And if this appears dismal from a scientific standpoint, from our own it is something to be celebrated: a final fascination in what certain unrepeatable lives found excellent, true, and real in the one life given to them to live. If there is a long and noble tradition of abstract thinkers, the present chapter would like to argue that that is but one choice; there is another domain, life itself, which is well capable of including within it as one possibility even the most abstract of concerns. *It raises the question* why anyone should choose "one is one" for a model of comprehension or an essential aim in existence. But it remains a question and not an attack, except tangentially, and therefore considers rational philosophy, taken seriously, as but one option and only one. The *alternative* would widen the diameter of the circle I spoke of earlier to include chaos, and would put the self at the center.\*

° These matters are developed in greater detail in my *Autobiographical Consciousness* (New York: Quadrangle Press, 1972).